THE RUSSIANS OF THE SOUTH.

Fa 190/4n2Q1

THE

RUSSIANS OF THE SOUTH.

BY

SHIRLEY BROOKS.

LONDON:

LONGMAN, BROWN, GREEN, AND LONGMANS.

1854.

RUSSIANS OF THE SOUTH.

CHAPTER I.

I was desirous to reach the Black Sea as speedily as possible, for I had marked out a long Oriental journey, to follow a visit to South Russia. But steam-boat arrangements delayed me for some days at Vienna, and there is perhaps no city (shall I, in grateful memory of the kaleidoscopic brightness and variety of Caireen *tableaux*, make one exception?) where an impatient traveller finds ampler atonement for being hindered on his way.

After a day's sight-seeing, conducted in that hard-working, persevering style adopted by English travellers, and neither exactly understood nor violently admired by foreigners, there are many less pleasant places than the front of a Viennese coffee-house to rest in. Seated at your little table, in the open air, with coffee, ice, or what you will, brought you at the slightest gesture to the sedulous and watchful attendants; with your *meerschaum*, or cigar, or *chibouque*, if you please—for there is too various and constant an influx of foreigners for any body to stare at any thing you may do; the darkening fortifications of the city before you, the brightening lights of the *café* behind you, and around you a miscellaneous group of officers in white uniform; full-dressed theatre-goers, taking their coffee *en route;* among them, perhaps, a few ladies; shabby artists, with terrible beards; sallow Jews, with keen eyes, watching every thing; a calm

B

Oriental, with a courteous gesture if you approach him, but apparently watching nothing; two or three full-blown, sunburnt English travellers, shouting out their half-dozen words of German with bold, insular intonation, and obviously conceiving that they are paying rather a graceful compliment to Austria by calling the waiter *Kellner;* a straggling Italian boy or two, with plaster medallions for sale; a batch of students, with belted *blouses;* and two or three mendicants, winding in and out among tables,— intruders whom an English waiter would bully off in two minutes, but for whom the Austrian waiter actually steps aside; —with this group, and a constant background of figures passing and repassing in the moonlight, you can amuse your eye very satisfactorily, while you rest your legs after your long walk to, and over, and round the lovely Leopoldsberg, or its neighbour, the Kahlenberg. And, if you like to talk, the only difficulty in the way of that is your probable ignorance of the language of your neighbour; but you may be quite sure that, if you address him, he will not edge away *Anglo-Saxonicè*, as much as to say, " I don't see why that fellah should address me."

At Vienna you purchase, from the agent of the Danube steam-boat company, a ticket, which costs you rather more than five pounds, and which entitles you to travel to Galatz. Your heavier luggage is taken from you, and a receipt for it given, which enables you to claim it at the end of the journey. The prudent traveller will of course have a small *sac de nuit* for the daily necessaries of the toilet—it will be seen presently under what favourable auspices that ceremony is performed on the Danube. Your embarkation takes place at some distance from the city, and the first day's journey occupies about three hours. This brings you to Presburg, where, according to your historic lights, you can recall the memories of Maria Theresa, or of the Bohemian girl. Instinctively anxious to defer sleeping on board the boat, until compelled to remain there, you will probably arrange, as I did, to pass the night at an hotel. At dinner I had a good deal of conversation with some officers in the white coats of Austria. They discussed the affairs of the world with a decision only equalled by the inexactness of their information.

But they were very gentlemanly and good-natured, and we got along capitally. One of them was a medical man, and peculiarly energetic upon all subjects. His zeal amused his friends, who once or twice evinced anxiety to impress upon me that his vehemence was only manner, and that he meant nothing rude. A band began to play outside, and struck up a march from *Robert le Diable*.

"Meyerbeer is liked in England, I think?" said one of the officers.

"Yes," I said; "so much so, that his three operas alone have carried one of our theatres through a brilliant season."

"He is an abominable man, and a blasphemer," remarked the medical gentleman; "and I should have great pleasure in meeting him in a boat."

While the others laughed, I was trying to explain to myself the logic of this choice of a nautical companion.

"Yes, assuredly," continued he. "You may laugh, gentlemen, but the whole object of that man's life is the overthrow of religion. All his works are wicked; but his last, *Le Prophète*, is the worst of all. He is a Jew, you know; that accounts for it."

"There can be no wickedness in music," said another, "and, therefore, you must refer to the words. Now, M. Scribe is not a Jew."

"No; but Meyerbeer tells him what to write. 'Write me,' says he, 'an attack on the Christian religion.' Scribe has no faith—what Frenchman has any? He doesn't care what he writes, so that he is paid. So out comes blasphemy like the *Prophète*, ridiculing our religion. I should like to meet M. Meyerbeer in a boat; it would give me much happiness."

"But why in a boat?"

"Because I would take him by his neck, and put him under the water. If I had him in a boat, we should have no more blasphemy from M. Meyerbeer."

My experiences of the rest of the night lead me to predict the following future. You will retire to your bed-room, and order the *fille de chambre* (a very dirty old man) to call you at four, as the boat starts at five. The bed is, of course, damp, but as you will throw yourself upon it dressed, that is of little consequence; but if you prudently cast the one sheet away, it falls upon the boards of the floor with a slapping weighty sound, like any other wet towel. Soon after two, the dirty old man will knock you up, and in answer to your vituperative eloquence, and your pointing to the real hour on your watch, will grumble angrily at your complaint about a trifle, and will walk out, wringing his hands furiously, and leaving the door open. Your sleep is broken, and you may as well go down-stairs. All the house is closed except the large billiard-room, which is lighted up, and upon the seats around which scores of passengers are lying, in every attitude of slumber except one of comfort. The sound of the snoring is varied by the smart clack of billiard balls, which are being knocked about by four or five Jew boys, who, relying on the sleepiness of the waiters, have stepped in through the open windows for a little cheap practice. An elderly officer is trying to read the *Wanderer* journal, and hits recklessly with his pipe-handle at any young Jew who may run between him and the lamps. A brilliant moonlight, streaming on the trees outside, presents ideas of coolness and freshness which render unbearable the mixture of heat, snoring, bad odours, and boys; and you walk about Presburg until the bell summons you either to a stifling cabin, which is worse than the billiard-room, or to a wet deck, around which the mists of the Danube steam heavily up. A cigar enables you to defy the lesser evil, and you remain on deck.

That day's voyage—a tolerable breakfast and an intolerable dinner by no means included in the passage money, but charged for at a price which would be high if the meals were good—brings you to Pesth. You would naturally go to La Reine Victoria— that is, "loyally you would, but physically you can't," because that once superbly placed hotel perished in the bombardment. But Pesth has abundance of other inns, some of them enormous. It seems a hard saying, but the fish of the Danube are almost the only really good things connected with that river. At six in the morning you are again on the wet deck. That night you reach Mohacs. But there is no going on shore to-night. At half-past eight the crowded cabin of the boat evinces symptoms of excitement, and the dirty, bearded waiters begin to be almost active, a symptom heretofore unseen. They suddenly snatch the table-cloth from before you, like the Wizard of the North doing a feat, and try to take away your tumbler of tea before you have finished it. With execrations, vented without the slightest respect for the affrighted company, every waiter commands all the others to move the tables; and after a quarter of an hour's wrangling, and great beating and hammering of the furniture, a work is effected which a couple of silent, handy English servants would have done in three minutes without attracting much observation. The tables are piled along the middle of the cabin. You sink back upon the seat which runs round the room, and admire the clumsiness with which the work has been done; if the vessel should rock ever so little, that upper table must come down—you hope upon your opposite neighbour's legs, you fear upon your own. A nearer danger threatens the latter. Your knees are suddenly plucked asunder by a waiter, who instantly dives down between them, and rests his shock head upon your lap. He fumbles beneath the seat, and drags out a sliding apparatus, which adds to that seat a pleasing slope of about four feet. Upon this he places—no, at this he throws (*you* may place it, if you like)—an exceedingly thin horse-hair cushion. Your bed is "made." Look round, and twenty-six other beds have been also "made," and the cabin suddenly resembles the ward of an hospital, except in that the ward is clean and quiet. But there are more than twenty-seven people here—you counted forty at dinner—where is the balance (as the Americans say) to sleep? Now, what *is* that to you? *you* have got a bed. But the ladies, will they not retire? Do the ladies interfere with you? No. But there is a very stout gentleman disarraying himself —he has taken off his coat, and his waistcoat, and his boots— yes, and his socks; and even yet you are not sure that he will disrobe no further. Well, the traveller on the Danube should learn to mind his own business.

Two hours pass, and now take a bird's-eye view of the cabin, but don't go out into the fresh air to return for that purpose, or you will never be able to endure the vile atmosphere on coming back.   Every body is what is amusingly called " in bed." The ladies have unhooked the backs of their dresses, and some of them have slipped off their shoes, and put on French nightcaps of great elegance, and they lie either in groups or alternating with the rougher voyagers.   Four or five of them are tittering together, unawed by the indignant grunts of the old people who want to go to sleep.   A Jewess, of very large size, has made prey of two cushions, and is fighting for her extra comfort with a snuffy old Italian, who has not one, having been asleep when the distribution took place.   Neither can speak the other's language, but they tug viciously at the cushion.   An Hungarian officer, for whom the bed is exactly half long enough, has built himself a sort of suspension bridge continuation with camp-stools, and they reach far across the cabin.   His opposite neighbour, a facetious and spectacled German, has been trying to steal the foremost stool, and much guttural abuse follows.   The floor is covered with sleepers, who, as they have the floor-cloth for a sheet, and nothing for a counterpane, may hereafter remember the night.   On the right is an Englishman, suffering martyrdom from the heat and the odour, but amid his sufferings preserving his English propriety, and sedulously occupied in preventing an elderly Polish lady, fast asleep, from becoming the unconscious sharer of his couch, into which she has rolled half a dozen times—while his boot is ceaselessly engaged in kicking his other neighbour, a Swedish watchmaker, who pillows his slumbers on his box of watches, and continues to emit perfect volleys of snorting.   Indeed the noise, when the passengers are asleep, is considerably greater than when they are all awake and sulky.   The cabin is lighted by means of one of the dinner tumblers, into which some oil and a floating wick have been placed—all the windows are closed, and also the door; but this last means of ventilation would have been open, but that the chief waiter, on being ordered to leave it so, loudly refused, on the ground that he and his friends were going to sup at the foot of the cabin stairs, and therefore he banged the door to, with great indignation. And sup they did, five of them, and chattered and laughed for a good hour, besides perfuming the greater part of the room with the savour of their steaming and rancid viands. The Englishman bears it as long as he can, but human endurance has its limits; and at length, roused from a hot doze by a scream from the large Jewess, from under whose proportions, as she slept, the wily Italian has plucked the cushion of strife, he bestows a last spurring upon the snorting Swedish watchmaker—dislodges the sleeping Polish lady from his side—and, tumbling over the vast length of the Hungarian officer, gains the deck, and outwatches the stars.

Such is a night on the Danube, and such are the comforts to which tourists, ladies included, are invited by the Austrian Company. I may be reminded that there is a lady's cabin—to which I shall reply that I not only know it, but that I examined it, and that its discomforts were as great as those of the larger cabin, while its atmosphere was worse than that of the latter. The simple fact is, that the affair is a monopoly, and that the conductors of the boats, eager to gain as much profit as possible, and fearless of opposition, crowd the vessels with as many persons as can be induced to enter them, and evince an utter disregard for the condition of those who have no appeal.

Such a night, and then another day's steaming—and Belgrade is reached. Gazing on the ruined and wretched place on the following morning, and remembering Croly's lines on the death of Czerni George, who in the last heroic rapture thought only of his Servian triumphs—

> ———"Nor saw
> The hurried glare of the Pacha,
> Nor saw the headsman's backward leap
> To give his blade the wider sweep"—

an *apropos* vision of a real Pacha suddenly appeared, attended by a distinguished suite. It required no great stretch of imagination, as the stern-looking silent old man came slowly on board, to believe that he had just left the scene of the execution, and that "the bloody head of the Pandour," on whose lips the "selfsame smile" of triumph was "lingering," would follow in the hands of the pikeman.   But these slaughterous notions were quickly dispelled by the behaviour of his Excellency (one of the uncles of the present Sultan,) who, after steadily and solemnly performing his devotions, like a man who was not ashamed of owning a God, proceeded to the next sacred duty of hospitality, and gave some of us cups of Turkish coffee.

But all that had hitherto marked the voyage, in the way of discomfort and delay, was a *bagatelle* compared to what followed. To call any of the incidents of the journey hardships would be misusing a term.   Of downright honest hardships any man who has been a sportsman must have voluntarily and cheerfully endured more in a week's Highland work, than he would meet in the whole Danube run.   But the voyage from Vienna to Skela Gladova, at least, is a series of annoyances and nuisances caused by avarice and negligence, and suggestive of all kinds of abominations, moral and physical.   Here is the remainder.

At four o'clock in the afternoon of the day on which we left Belgrade, the boat came to a standstill.   I was about to say that the captain explained that he could go no farther—but he thought no such courtesy worth his trouble, and the same want of ordinary civility was constantly conspicuous on the part of other servants of these boats.   But this is a trifle.   We suddenly stopped in a solitary part of the river, where no house, nor even station, gave indication of human inhabitants.   And we learned, by cross-examining the sailors, that there was not water enough to float us farther.   Then we must go on in some sort of conveyances—where were they?   It was early, and there were two good hours of light.   I observed that at this reasonable suggestion looks were exchanged between the captain and an official called "the conductor," and the latter went on shore, saying that he was going to procure conveyances for us.   "Procure," thought I, absurdly bringing ideas of English business habits into connection with such people; "why are they not ready?   The people hereabouts must have known—it is their business to know—whether the boat could proceed."   It did not occur to me that the fellow had not the remotest intention of getting conveyances. But so it was.   We waited, and it grew dusk, and then dark;

and then the waiters told us with grins that we should not move that night, but that early in the morning there would be a "barge" for us. It was raining heavily, and there was nothing to do but to growl and submit.

Between four and five in the morning, we were roused from the charming couches I have described, and were further informed that we had better make haste. This was certainly needless, as no one can accuse a traveller by a Danube steamboat of wasting time over the minor coxcombries of the toilet. Seeing that there is no kind of provision for the ceremony of ablution (except an atrocious corner in a gloomy closet, where there is something resembling a basin, but seldom any water, though this is the less to be regretted, as soap and towels are unknown)—but that the persevering Sybarite who insists in going through the form, can only do so by dipping the corner of his handkerchief into a tumbler of muddy water—about two minutes is amply sufficient for all libations to the Graces. And being ready, we were hurried, breakfastless, upon the soaking deck, and over the side into the barge. This was a newly painted affair, and was therefore clean, at all events. It consisted of one low cabin, about twenty feet long. At one end of this was an area of some ten feet, which might be termed the after-deck—it contained the wheel and the helmsman. The other end was occupied by the rowers, of whom at that hour we could, of course, see nothing. A vast mass of baggage and luggage had been piled in the centre of the cabin, and around it the majority of passengers contrived to find standing room; and hot as the place was, and reeking with the fresh paint, it was a degree better than the abominable steamer.

We were rowed for three hours, and, between the intervals of the rain, we could see that we were passing through fine hill scenery; but the position was not favourable for making any observations—except a few upon the steam-packet company. But about eight o'clock the sky cleared, and the passengers, ravenous with hunger, would have demanded food, but that there was no one of whom to demand it. The only servant of any description on board was the steersman, and he had enough on his hands in swearing at the rowers, who were the wretchedest of Hungarian peasants, apparently half-starved, and at least half naked. His incessant and voluminous objurgations were perfectly overwhelming; but when the passengers found that there was literally nothing whatever to eat or drink, I fear that some of them began to take the work of commination out of his hands. Others, more practical, landed, and rushed into a village—if half a dozen huts and a wretched *gast-haus* can be called a village—and sought to levy contributions upon the inhabitants. How others fared there was no time to ascertain; but for myself, after examining the contents of every larder in the whole place, I felt happy in securing a lump of damp, black bread, a great piece of strong cheese, and a draught of wine, at whose relationship to vinegar it would be ungrateful, under the circumstances, to hint. Thus provisioned, I and others returned to the barge, which we then found was utterly deserted. Concluding that the crew had retired to refresh themselves, we waited in tolerably silent patience for one hour—and again in patience, if not quite so silent, for another hour. It was then considered expedient to make a few inquiries, as affairs began to look as if we were designed to form an involuntary colony on the banks of the Danube. The village, being small, was easily searched by a determined party, and our late captain, helmsman, pilot, or what you will, was discovered in a chimney smoking his cigars. He seemed happy, but affected sorrow, which was not affected on his auditors' part when the state of matters was disclosed. The rowers had revolted. They had brought us to Drenkova, and then, conceiving us at their mercy, had refused to proceed unless an enormous addition were made to their pay. The captain had declined to vary the bargain, and the peasants had dispersed, leaving the boat *planté*. "It was abominable." Herein we agreed, including the company's arrangements in the adjective. "But we *must* go on." The captain, not being disputatious, admitted the abstract fact, but did not see how the matter was to be managed. He had done all he could—he had sent into some other villages to see whether other rowers could be obtained —he hoped they would come—and did any gentleman want "fire" for his cigar? Again there was no appeal. We remained as we were, in sulkiness, for another hour. Then we became outrageous, and an American gentleman casually mentioned, that in the box upon which he was sitting there was a revolving pistol with six barrels. This afforded us some comfort, and we decided upon another charge upon the captain.

He was slightly advanced in liquor, but was obviously transacting business—which was consolatory, as we had now lost four hours, and the mid-day sun was scorching into our very brains. He ordered four peasants to do something. I do not think they could have understood his orders with precision, for they all came and sat down in a row upon the shore, looking at the barge. We assisted at this operation for some time, and then forcibly dragged the captain to the spot. He approached the nearest of the men, and, to do him justice, gave him one of the most tremendous kicks which ever awakened a gentleman to a sense of his duty. A loud hurrah from the Anglo-Americans instantly rewarded this exhibition of firmness. The effect was remarkable. In five minutes a large open barge was moored alongside our own—the four men, shouting, scrambling, screaming, and swearing, began to transfer the luggage from the latter to the former—the smallest chip boxes, ladies' parasols, workbaskets, packets of *galanterie*, and other fragile matters, were flung in first, and vast trunks, portmanteaus, and an actual chest of drawers, were hauled down upon them—the scrunching being distinctly heard by the terrified owners of the lighter ware; a black canvass was drawn over the whole, and the four men, seizing oars, went away with their spoil, nobody knew whither. But something was done, and the plundered passengers looked cheerfully at one another.

Half an hour more, and there was a rush; the captain sprang in at the end of the boat, and eight peasants, a trifle more starved and naked than their predecessors, but who seemed to us models of energy and manly vigour, crowded in at the other. The barge was cast off; the skilful steersman shifted the helm, the faithful fellows with the oars pulled gallantly, and in not more than five hours from the time we had "sighted" Drenkova, we were taking a last sight at that remarkable locality. It did not look half so wretched now that we were going away. "We shall reach Orsova to-night," said we, "and sleep there, and to-morrow for the Iron Gate and the large steamer at Skela Gladova." We forgot our miserable fare, and made up our minds to enjoy the remainder of the voyage. After all, we said, delays will occur, and Hungarians will revolt, and if the villagers had possessed any better food, they would certainly have sold it to us. And so we moved on slowly, but not sulkily, and the gentleman with the revolving pistol was silently considered as little better than a very unscrupulous character. We climbed upon the top of the cabin, and sat upon the little deck, and told one another marvels of other lands, with more or less of truth in them. Our good-humour was a little marred by finding, that at the next village at which we rested there were exactly the same provisions to be obtained as at Drenkova—black bread, strong cheese, and sour wine;· but we remembered that our journey would soon be over, and we thought of the fleshpots of Orsova, and rejoiced.

The wind rose, and the captain declared that the bodies of the passengers upon the roof of the cabin and on deck caught it, and interfered with the rowing; he therefore commanded that we should all descend into the said cabin, and remain there until further orders. There was some show of reason in this, and he was obeyed by the men, but many of the ladies refused to move. It was now observed that the rowers were doing nothing—their oars were lifted lightly from the water a few inches, and dropped in again, but there was no pulling. This was remarked to the captain, who was kind enough to swear at them a good deal, but without much effect. Day was closing, and awful apprehensions came upon us, which deepened as we glided into a grim gorge of overhanging mountains. What if we are unable to proceed further! No beds, no food, no fire. An hour or so were passed while every body was abusing every body else for talking such nonsense. Keep us in this thing all night! The captain would not dare to do it! But the captain, like Macheath, was "a bold man," and he did it. About eight o'clock in a pitch-dark night we were made fast to another stump, and were informed that in all probability we should *not* be able to proceed next day. The American gentleman was unseasonably facetious, and remarked that we were also made fast in another way. What scraps of black bread were left to us were selfishly hoarded, each passenger denying that he had any thing. We now felt fairly abandoned by fortune, in a dismal mountain gorge, in darkness, and with nothing to eat; there was even no lying down to die, for the space was so confined that any gentleman desirous to depart this life must have done so like the Roman Emperor—" standing."

The Turks in the suite of the Pacha—for his excellency had chartered a private barge, and nobody knew where he was —had scrambled on shore, and, climbing up the rocks till they found a soft place, had kindled a fire, and were soon squatting around it, making coffee. The red glow of their fire—bringing out their picturesque dresses in bright colour amid the jet black of the night, and fitfully glancing into the awful-looking caves and chasms in the precipitous and overarching crags — was noticeable, amid our misery and malignity. They also sent us coffee, which was a charitable act, and deserves record. They repeated this kindness in the morning. I am afraid that sundry on board contrasted the conduct of the Christians of the steam-boat company with that of the Mohammedans of the rocks, very much to the disadvantage of the former.

As had been predicted, the wind was high in the morning, and the wretched barge could not proceed. The tiniest steam-tug, of one Shetland-pony power, then lying among the creeks of Rotherhithe, would have saved all these hours of delay and discomfort. So we said, angrily nudging into the cabin, the rain pouring in a deluge. It was some comfort to see that the captain was wetter than I ever saw a man before; I should think he must have been actually limp with that morning's soaking. I believe that at last he could bear the infliction no longer; for the wind was just as high as ever at one o'clock, when he rose from deck, and, streaming like a river-god, ordered the rowers to pull. They did so, and we growled all the louder, that the order had not been given earlier, for in three hours we were at

Orsova. If the passengers paid for all they ate during the first two hours after their rush upon the town, the innkeepers and others—for we ran into every house we saw, and listened to no reclamations—must have realized a goodly competence. That night we slept in beds; it had not recently happened, nor did it soon happen again.

In the morning there was much trouble about passports—that abomination of the Continent; those who had received the due *visé* were graciously permitted to continue their journey, but all were not so fortunate. Two poor young ladies—Venetians, going to Bukarest—had some informality detected by the military commandant, and were refused permission to proceed. Four or five days must elapse before they could hear from the last place where the passport had been examined. I do not think the poor girls had much more money than was necessary for the mere journey, and here was nearly a week's lodging and living to be added. To be sure, it would have been a dreadful thing if they had departed with an imperfect passport, and had conspired, and overthrown the government with their crochet needles. We left them sobbing together on their big box, in a bye-lane leading to the wharf. The luggage was examined here, and as there is a duty upon articles of *galanterie*—those knick-knacks which ladies buy, and which are given them, or which they win at raffles, exchange with one another, or otherwise obtain in a variety of innocent ways— the lady luggage was mercilessly scrutinized. All the tiny red boxes, and bead purses, and ring cases, and housewives, *bon-bon* baskets, and jewel caskets, and the hundred little lurking-places in which woman hides her poor little treasures, were remorselessly turned out by big-bearded fellows with grubby nails, grinned over, and thrust back roughly, or seized, as the case might be. I have seen a good deal of custom-house work, but I never saw the female *paraphernalia* so closely scrutinized. The masculine luggage seemed to pass more easily, except as regarded books, which terrify these people dreadfully. It was a long time before I could get a volume of Mr. Dickens' out of the officer's paws; I think I finally succeeded by some pantomime, tending to induce the belief that it was a work of devotion, and necessary to my observance of religious duties.

Being at Orsova, and a few miles only from Skela Gladova, which is below the Iron Gate, with one's passport *visé* and one's shirts ransacked, it might be hoped that we were likely to advance a little. It was now nine in the morning—the day was before us. But for three hours after all was ready, we did nothing. The conveyances which were to take us to Skela Gladova were assembled, but the police forbade us even to enter them until they gave the signal. So we lounged about on the muddy wharf of Orsova until that signal came. The conveyance was not a carriage, nor a fly, nor even the humble omnibus; but it was a fusty wicker basket, placed upon four rotten wheels, without springs and without seats, though containing a good deal of damp hay to lie upon. A sort of thatch over it housed a good many spiders, but it also kept off some of the rain. There were about thirty of these waggons, and at the good pleasure of the police we all scrambled into them, and hoped we were going. Not so fast. Every driver, before he dared give his horse the initiative cut, was compelled to be furnished with a ticket. And this the police would not give him, if there were fewer or more than three passengers in his vehicle. Now, as we had not naturally divided ourselves into leashes, there was a good half-hour's work, quarrelling and scuffling, pulling extra people out and forcing extra people in, and exchanging abuse with those who had secured comfortable places, and refused to stir. At last we all went off together, the horses going very fast, and we rushed upon some green turf, along which we went in capital style for at least a quarter of a mile. Here were we stopped by sentinels, and every driver had to descend, and get another passport for himself *and his horse*, whose colour was carefully examined, and accurately noted. For all these men belong to the Austrian military frontier, and are in fact a militia, and not one must be allowed to escape. About an hour being thus spent, we started again. The next step was to examine our own passports, for the last time in Austria. We were approved, all but three of us, and these were sent back. The remainder crossed a bridge, and were out of Austria.

No great thanks for that—for instantly, on entering Wallachia, we had a very long examination indeed. I think we must have been sitting in front of the guard-house at Werezerowa nearly two hours, while some of the stupidest functionaries I ever quarrelled with were vainly trying to understand the American gentlemen's passports, which, for some reason not easily given, are always in English. Our own foreign secretary, addressing Continental readers, wrote—more sensibly, I think—in a language they were likely to comprehend. But at last we got away, and the drivers flogged their horses well, and forced them into quick trot. The rain came down; so did the spiders; but that was nothing. The crazy vehicles, of which only two broke down (mine was not one,) went over the ground in excellent style and though every bone in one's body was sore with the jolting, and three days did not efface the recollection, we all ran, drenched, but in good temper, into the cabin of the large and commodious steamer, the Arpad, which lay waiting us at Skela Gladova.

So ended all the real annoyances of the journey; for though the Arpad lost much time, and many a fine hour of light during which we might have made way—and though the captain informed us that we should lose the Russian boat at Galatz, and be compelled to wait at that pestiferous hole for a fortnight, or to journey 190 miles to Odessa in a cart like those we had just left—yet, as this prediction proved untrue, and the boat did wait, he may be forgiven the annoying anticipations he caused us. They only show the want of system, knowledge, and habits of business prevalent on the line of journey. But the accommodations were so tolerable, and the general management of this part of the voyage so superior, that few of the passengers, on reaching Galatz, hesitated to sign the testimonial inserted in the packet's book by the American traveller, namely, that, " considering the atrocious and infernal character of our treatment *above* Skela Gladova, we are very happy to express our satisfaction with the Arpad." The officials doubtless obliterated the inscription in the book as soon as they were enabled to comprehend its bearing—as I observed they had previously done in reference to all other than complimentary remarks.

It only remains to add, that the luggage and passengers for Odessa are transferred—the former without examination, the latter after their passports have been twice examined in the abominable town of Galatz (whose indescribable filth exceeds the power of imagination)—from the Austrian to the Russian boat, another packet awaiting those for Constantinople. The egress from the Danube is by the Sulineh mouth, the only outlet for large vessels. If, after what I have said, an English traveller selects the Danube for his Continental trip, he will do so with his eyes open—though I dare not promise him that he will conclude it in the same state; for unless he is luckily late, as I was, when the cold has begun to set in, he will probably have the additional pleasure of being bitten blind and driven half mad by the mosquitoes.

The journey from the single Moldavian port, Galatz, to the Sulineh mouth of the Danube, and thence across a corner of the Black Sea, up to Odessa, is performed in a Russian steam-boat, with which no reasonable man can find any fault. This latter portion of the voyage is usually achieved in about twenty-four hours, unless the elements—represented by a strong wind, forcing back into the narrow jaws of the Danube so much of its water as to leave an insufficient depth upon the bar—are imperative in their opposition. The Russian boat is well officered, and its commanders, naval and military, have some sense of the value of an article upon which foreigners habitually set little store—I mean time. Affairs are conducted on board her with a determination and precision strongly contrasting with the system in the Austrian river service. I am glad to bear my testimony to the merits of the old Peter the Great, a vessel fitted with English engines, and graced with more warlike appurtenances in the form of a couple of brass guns, trophies of the earliest of the victories of the Prince Woronzow— a nobleman who has so many claims to the regard of Englishmen, and who has done so much good wherever he has had authority, that one is sorry to be compelled to hope that he will gain few additional honours in the struggle he is now conducting on the part of Russia.

c

CHAPTER II.

ODESSA is a new town. The Turks had formerly a fortress here, which was called Khodja Bey, and was taken from them by Catherine the Second, the wife of Peter the Third, and patroness of Don Juan. It pleased her truculent majesty to call the place Odessus, since which time the name has taken its more Italianized sound. I need not remark that the town stands upon the Black Sea, but I may observe that it is so placed in a bay that, looking upon the sea, you look north, Constantinople being in fact behind you—a circumstance which would not occur to you from a glance at the map. The town stands well, and its appearance from the sea is striking ; its cliffs, which are bold, being crowned by white buildings of considerable size, and some of which have a classical character. The most prominent of these is the mansion of Prince Woronzow, distinguished by a cluster of columns detached from the house, and forming an ornamental erection to which the eye is instantly attracted. The next object which strikes you is a gigantic staircase, consisting of nearly two hundred steps, leading directly down from the centre of the town to the beach. This was constructed a few years ago by the Prince. An elegant statue of the Duc de Richelieu (a French emigrant, who became the exemplary governor of Odessa, devoted himself to its improvement, and died in honourable poverty) stands at the head of the staircase ; but, seen from below, it is crushed by the vast proportions of the latter, and should have been colossal, or placed elsewhere. Odessa is of great extent. Its streets are broad, and though many of them are precipitous, and all which are paved are insufficiently paved, their general effect is good. There is a museum and a public library, and there are also an opera-house and "national" theatres. The state of the streets is the first great eyesore to an Englishman. The dust is so plentiful that the slightest breeze covers you with white powder, as if you had been paying a visit to a mill, and at times the clouds are so dense that the opposite houses can hardly be discerned. When rain falls matters are even worse, and the sojourner at Odessa is in mud to the ankles. There is a newspaper here, the *Journal d'Odessa*, but it is beneath contempt; the censorship prevents its containing any real information, and its critical articles are the very washiest of French flippancies. The language of business here is to a great extent Italian, but you hear almost every tongue under heaven in the course of a stroll through the port or Custom-house. The names of all the streets are written in Russ, with an Italian version below.

But Odessa, as a large but dull town, and Odessa as a busy port, with the flags of all nations rising from the double clump of masts—those in quarantine, and those "free"—are two distinct places. Odessa is the great focus into which is concentrated the result of the agricultural industry of the Southern Russian empire. Wheat, the chief representative of that industry, is here delivered from enormous distances, to be poured into the ships which have crossed the Black Sea to receive it. It is collected from a vast extent of country; and both water and land carriage are employed to transmit it to the harbour of Odessa. England, France, Spain, Denmark, Sardinia, Naples, Sweden, Sicily, and Turkey—all, according to their respective needs, send vessels to fetch the wheat thus gathered. The place itself has little or no actual connection with agriculture. Situated without the dreary waste called a Steppe (known to the ancients by the name of *Sors Deserta*,) the town is not devoid of patches of land where something approaching to fertility may be occasionally witnessed. But scarcely has the traveller's foot left the widely extended and wretchedly paved streets, on his progress inland, than he finds himself in the desert of the Steppe. "From the sea," says a writer of authority, "to the northern limit of the Steppe which surrounds the shores of the Black Sea, from the mouths of the Dniester to those of the Don, is a distance varying in extent, of about 100 English miles. Most parts of this Steppe are said to be calculated, with moderately good husbandry, for the cultivation of wheat; but there is a want of water, and no trees grow upon it. From February to May the grass is most luxuriant; but in the latter month it begins to wither, and in the summer the land is so totally deprived of all verdure as to present the picture of a dry sand bank on the sea shore."

As, therefore, this desert barrier at present prevents the existence of agriculture within a vast distance from Odessa, it will be seen that this insulated, handsome, and important town is a mere mouth—a gigantic trough, down which is perpetually streaming the "golden grain" of half an empire.

The comparative position of the various classes in Odessa will be better understood, if the scale of accommodations and conveniences required by the social habits of the place be in some measure explained. The dwelling-house is, of course, the most ordinary and useful test of position.

The highest style of abode presented by Odessa is the palace of the noble. The lowest is one which, though I have examined it with great care, and in various places, I find a difficulty in describing by any other name than the "tub" of the fruit-woman. The first would do honour to any capital in Europe—the inhabitants of the second are not Troglodytes, and that is all. Between these two extremes ranges every variety of residence, the diversity being, I think, more considerable, and the distinct types more numerous, than in any other large town with which I am acquainted. The gradual slope from the extreme of luxury to the extreme of squalor is not marked by the broad gaps which separate class from class with us; but the residences appear gradually to get a little less commodious, and then a little worse, and then worse still, and so on, until by an undisturbed process you find yourself transferred from the palace to the Diogenean home I have mentioned. There is, of course, a reason for every thing; and the reason, in the present case, is to be found in the remarkable variety of the population, which, representing almost every nation on earth, has adapted its domiciliary comforts to accordance with its strangely differing needs and customs.

The town, exceedingly spacious, is laid out with great regularity, and with a width of street which will leave little complaint to the sanitary reformers of future days, should such mischievous persons ever be admitted into Russia. The streets, from the nature of the ground, are in many cases precipitous, and the wretched state of the paving adds to the discomfort of the pedestrians. The best paving is where small rough stones are placed closely, as this affords a foot-hold in wet weather. Elsewhere there is a narrow line of slabs, running down the middle of the trottoir (if one may so use the word,) the right and left of this strip being left untouched. Beyond this, and between what ought to be the kerb and the carriage-way, is the drainage of Odessa—a bricked channel, about two feet deep, open at the top, and with which the houses communicate by similar but smaller channels, crossing the foot-way, but usually covered with a board. As these larger channels turn the corners of the streets, it is frequently necessary to cross them, to the continuous disgust of the organ usually affected by such places, while the eye is also constantly annoyed by very loathsome sights. The carriage way is unspeakably rough in most parts, and the traveller in one of the ordinary vehicles of the town, which dash about with a headlong audacity, delightful to behold from a safe place, has frequent cause to execrate the road over which he is tearing. So much for paving and draining. The lighting of this large town is worthy of the other arrangements. The residence of one hundred thousand people, and the site of a dozen palaces, has no gas. There is a series of oil lamps, which serve to mark out the corners of the streets, and occasionally to preserve the pedestrian from an open drain, but these are miserably insufficient. There is a sort of excuse offered for the absence of paving; the stone of the district is too soft, and the experiment of asphalte fails in consequence of the alternately intense heat and cold, while the real paving slab cannot be procured nearer than Trieste. For people who believe in excuses this may serve; an inconsiderate Englishman might say, " Very well, fetch the slabs from Trieste," but this is not the

way in these parts.   But for the absence of gas there is no reason
at all, except that one which will ever oppose all improvement in
Russia.   The habit of bigoted or interested hostility to every
change, has repeatedly interfered when it has been endeavoured
to establish a gas manufactory; and so the inhabitants of Odessa
have gone on nightly breaking their shins, and tumbling into
their dirty drains, for want of an article which no respectable
English village is without.   The remaining feature of the streets
of Odessa is one to which I adverted in my first letter—the dust.
I may almost be suspected of dwelling upon a trivial matter; but
let the doubter visit Odessa, and let him walk down three streets
of the town in his Sunday black, and he will "see what then."
The dust lies like a universal shroud of some two or three inches
thick.   The slightest breeze flings it over the town in clouds, the
lightest footstep sends it flying high in dense heaps.   When,
therefore, I tell you that hundreds of the carriages of the places,
driven at high speed—the shaft horse in a rapid trot, and his
companion by his side in a showy canter—are perpetually racing
about, and that the sea breezes are as perpetually rushing
through the streets, the statement that Odessa lives in a cloud
is no figure of speech.   I have ventured a complaint or two,
when turning a corner I have suddenly found myself blinded,
and covered all over with a fine white powder, of which it is
very difficult to get rid, but my Odessa friends laugh, and say,
" Only wait and see a real dust-day.   This is nothing."   And I
am perfectly ready to believe that for hours together, as I am
told is the case, the houses on the other side of the street are
utterly invisible.   There are no water-carts; but I believe water
is considered to aggravate the evil, as it converts the dust into a
horrible mud, which, from the state of the "pavement," is almost
impassable.   Such are the comforts of the morning and evening
promenade in Odessa.

But it must not be assumed, from the indifference of the inhabitants to what we consider essential matters, that there is any
stagnation in the town.   On the contrary, every body is busy.
Building is going on in all directions, and upon a scale of great
magnitude.   Several noble palaces—the word is applicable from

the size and intended style of the new edifices—are in rapid course of erection. The soft stone to which I have alluded—and which is habitually cut and shaped with a small hatchet, like wood, but which hardens with exposure to the air—affords great facilities for building purposes. Small mountains of it, in a rough state, are to be seen at this moment in various corners of the town, and numerous stone-cutters are busily reducing it to the blocks required by the architect. Of the new buildings of a large description, some are to be the residences of members of the aristocracy—others are the property of wealthy tradesmen, and are intended to be let, either entire or in superb suites of apartments. One noble mansion, which I went over from court-yard to roof, is the property of an English merchant resident here, and will be one of the most splendid houses in the place. The stairs are of marble, and the walls of the principal apartments are also of a beautiful white marble, the effect of which, when polished, will be most brilliant. The carvings of the ceilings are elaborately tasteful, and the mahogany doors (costing here from sixty to seventy pounds each) will complete the rich character of the saloons. I mention these details to show the expensive mode in which building is carried on, the house I have referred to being by no means an extraordinary specimen of the Odessa style, which is carried to a more extravagant point in other mansions over which I have been taken.

Now for the contrast. In a department of the vast market, here called the Bazaar, and in which every conceivable article which is required for domestic consumption may be obtained, there is a wide space (fronting a burial-ground) where the vendors of fruit and vegetables chiefly congregate. The fruit season was nearly over, so that the display was of course much less brilliant than during the summer months. But here may be seen the articles used in culinary mysteries, in masses to which we are unaccustomed. A row of little hills of tomatas runs glowing and shining along one side of the market, while behind them rises a mountain chain of melons, in heaps breast high, around whose base roll, in humble subjection, scores of yellow-bellied pumpkins. Apples of every variety, vast and sallow, or

smaller and red as sunset, lie around you in thousands, filling
the air with their aroma, and reminding you of cider days in
pleasant villages at home. And as for the millions of onions, dried
beans, mushrooms hanging in mighty ropes, pears of a noble
juiciness and a sturdy flavour, purple plums of great size and ex-
cellence, and a hundred other vegetarian idols, it is difficult to
imagine how so many can have been brought together, and still
more difficult to imagine why. No population, even one of
schoolboys let loose with orders to be moderate, could make a
perceptible hole in those mighty stores.

The persons who preside over them have no affinity with
their wealthy hoards. The peasant here is a wretched-looking
being—dirty, ill-clad, and hungry-looking. His shaggy beard,
huge boots outside his trousers, dingy blue frock, and rough cap,
speak of hardships of all kinds. But give him his short black
pipe, and spirits enough to madden and then to stupefy him, and
he will not complain of his destiny. The female of the same
class is even more easily contented. The tub residences to which
I referred are among the features of the monster market here,
and they are inhabited by women. Elevation, ground-plan, and
other architectural contrivances, are all comprehended in a
single effort. A large black cask, somewhat resembling a sugar
hogshead, is laid on its side, and the house is built. A quantity
of hay is laid inside, and the house is furnished. The lady gets
in upon the hay, and the house is inhabited. Before the entrance of the mansion she strews the onions, tomatas, or whatever else she may vend, and during the hours of business she
sits in the tub, smokes her pipe, chaffers with her customers,
and says her prayers. After business is over she ascertains in
which quarter the wind sits—turns the closed end of her tub
towards that quarter, and creeps to rest in peace and tranquillity.
But some of these women are ambitious, and take to building.
They do not, indeed, demand marble staircases and mahogany
doors; but they take two tubs, which are laid face to face, at a
distance of three or four feet—and over the interstice, tubs and
all, is placed a watertight canvass. The fair occupant (and two
or three whom I saw, though not literally fair. were extremely

pretty) has then two rooms, besides a hall; but this luxury is not adopted by the older class, who think that we ought to adhere to the customs of our ancestors.

The dwelling of the workman I have also visited, in several of the suburbs. It has one or two features of a satisfactory character. It usually consists of a single-roomed cottage, in which the whole family resides, and in which all the domestic operations are carried on. But although the accommodation is so limited, I have observed in many of these cottages a disposition to cleanliness, or at all events such an avoidance of very gross uncleanliness, as is by no means habitual in this country. The furniture of the room—I will take one of those I have inspected as a type, it is a fair average specimen—is simple in the extreme. The great feature in it is the bed—a large structure, solidly made, and in which, I am informed, the Russian workman takes much pride. It was well kept, and, although it lacked the rich hue and fine polish which a hundred years of "elbow grease" in an English peasant's hereditary cottage gives to his household furniture, it spoke of cleanliness and attention. As for the mass of mattress and cushions piled upon it, that, too, was a feature, but a national one. To my taste, there appeared to be at least four times as much as was desirable; but these cottages are frail in construction, and the winter in Odessa is excessively severe. The remainder of the apartment was occupied by a small table, two or three stools, and a chair, whose fractures had been set and secured by thin strips of iron. Besides a 'white-faced baby (exceeding small, but with huge sparkling black eyes), which lay comfortably in its father's immense sheepskin coat, rammed with difficulty into a tiny cradle, so as to make the warmest of nests —and a few cooking utensils, there was nothing else to catalogue, if I except a vile coloured print of some saint, and a still worse woodcut of the Emperor (the two great objects of a Russian's worship), which shared the honours of the walls. Of the information given me by the inhabitant of this cottage, and by other men of a similar class, I shall speak in its proper place.

The habitations of the better class—who, however, are neither of the aristocracy nor of the mock aristocracy of the *bureau*—are very comfortable. Many of them are in houses surrounded by a court-yard, the gates of which are closed at night. The entrance does not give you an idea of the commodiousness within; for the door is usually approached by an insignificant or inconvenient staircase, with perhaps a verandah at the top. It is, however, something to be elevated from the court-yard, in which there is possibly a pool of stagnant water, and almost certainly a variety of heaps of garbage, the refuse of the different households, which squabbling dogs are littering about, or disputing with one another. It is well to see and smell as little as may be in such places. But once inside the house, and every thing is orderly and neat. The absence of fireplaces and carpets, except perhaps a scrap in the centre of the best room, is the only thing which indicates to you that you are not in England—unless, perhaps, that some of the engravings on the walls, usually French, are not what a prudent English husband and father would select for the adornment of his home. In other respects there is little to distinguish the tradesman's house in Odessa from that of his competitor in London.

The shops, however, have a marked difference from those of the French and English capitals. The windows are all small, and there is no attempt at display in them. Whatever there is to see must be sought inside. From this cause, and from the absence of gas, the shops of Odessa, especially at night, present a sombre and lugubrious aspect. There are good shops, but you must look for them. The shops, however, to which the custom of the poorer classes is invited, "hang out lights" (as Thomas Moore has it), by the display of signs of every kind. These pictorial invitations have not the artistic merit of the signs of Vienna, where one frequently sees a really able picture suspended as the indication of trade; but they have a boldness of conception and a strength of colour which adapts them to their public use. The favourite design is a hand, stretched forth from heaven, and grasping a cornucopia. From this is poured forth, as if supplied to the tradesman direct from Providence, a stream of whatever wares may be the object of his traffic. I think I have most frequently seen it at the shoemaker's, where I have remarked that from a small horn of plenty, apparently incapable of containing more than a pair of shoes (and thence the more miraculous), streams forth every species of foot-casing—the tremendous jack-boot, the delicate white slipper, the compromising high-low, the aristocratic pump, the blue tinted cloth boot, and even baby's pink worsted shoes, with fairy buckles. But the shoemaker is not the only pretender to celestial bounties. The baker has his cornucopia, and loaves of all kinds and shapes come down from heaven like manna—from the black bread, which would seem to require the digestion of an ostrich, to the delicious white loaf, which would do credit to the elegant "fancy baker." But the mere suggestion implied by the hand is despised by some bolder traders (who may perhaps be Mormonites), and an entire angel, with white wings and red legs, appears bodily in their devices, urging and enabling them to supply a desiring public with cigars, hammers and nails, or *votki*, as the case may be. I need not say that these outward and visible signs of the trades carried on within, are to a great extent necessary to a population not usually so lucky as the excellent *Dogberry* conceives mankind to be. "To be a well-favoured man is the gift of fortune, but to read and write comes by nature."

I have now, perhaps, succeeded in giving some idea of the general characteristics of the town. It would be more easy than profitable to devote more space to mere description, and there might be the advantage of novelty in such a course, as I am not aware that there is any satisfactory English account of a place which must be full of interest to so many Englishmen. But for my purpose it will be sufficient, as it is necessary, to say that the population of Odessa finds, in the united occupations provided by the port (of which I have still to speak), and by the town, amply sufficient employment. There is mendicancy here, but, so far as I have had an opportunity of observing, the beggars have been old men, obviously past all work, to whom law would elsewhere give an asylum. You find them sitting, sunning themselves, on the hillocks of stone around the new buildings, and as they pull off their hats and display broad bald heads, sometimes of a fine character, contrasting with the silvery beard and otherwise amply garnished face and throat, you are reminded of many of the Rembrandt portraits you have seen in your way hither. But these exceptional beggars cannot be considered a symptom of a system, in such a population as that of Odessa.

I shall have to refer to one more feature in the town which it would be unpardonable to pass over, and then I shall be at liberty to pass to the specific details which I have sought to collect. I shall proceed to give such a. statement of the mode of existence of the working man here, of his hours of labour, of the remuneration he receives, of the mode in which he is compelled to expend that remuneration, and the mode also in which his own habits induce him to spend it, as will enable a reader to draw his own comparison between the condition of a Russian and of an English workman. In treating this subject, and indeed to render some of its details intelligible, I shall occasionally be compelled to refer to the Russian system of commercial restriction and government interference. It exercises too obvious an influence upon the ordinary transactions of life to be overlooked. But I shall do so only when necessitated, as my concern is with facts and not with theories. I may add here, that although I am myself fortunate in possessing means of obtaining information upon many topics to which I shall advert, and therefore that I can claim no credit for simply availing myself of them, it is easy to see the difficulties under which an inquirer must labour in seeking to examine the workings of the Russian social system. There is so obvious a disinclination on the part of every official and *employé* to furnish any detail or information likely to be made public, that application to these gentlemen is merely throwing time away. Under an order from a superior they would in due time—that is, in the course of a very long time—produce any required returns; but it is neither the habit of their minds nor the etiquette of their offices to understand, far less to communicate, aught not prepared upon their own writing-tables. And although the independence of commercial life, and the spirit of intelligence which it demands, in a great measure does away with both these obstacles in the case of the mercantile public here, there is still a timidity and an unwillingness to be known as having furnished information, at which an Englishman has no right to smile, inasmuch as he cannot be acquainted with the ramifications by which official and other displeasure succeeds in reaching those whose conduct may have been unacceptable. There is no country in the world where secresy is so completely the order of the day as in Russia. Were it necessary I could mention curious instances in proof of this—any resident in Russia, if he dared, could confirm it. Of those social outrages, for instance, which our own press hastens to report with a minuteness and a frankness utterly incomprehensible to foreigners (who have incessantly on their lips, and in their practice, the celebrated dictum that one's *linge sale* should be washed " at home"), the Russian affects to know nothing, although they have occurred within a few miles of his doors. With us such outrages are placed either in the category of phenomena, or as signs of something wrong in a system; but not only is nothing ever wrong in Russia, but there are no phenomena. Every thing is orderly, regular, and loyal. If an agrarian crime in which many persons are accomplices is committed, a battalion is marched to the spot, every body is hurried away to Siberia; but there is no scandal. A Russian will deny to you that such a thing is possible, and how will you prove it? But the Russian, uttering his very denial, knows that the thing is not only possible, but that it has occurred.

"The Quarantine" at Odessa is one of the most curious features of the place, and it is one to which the resident earliest conducts the stranger, whether the visit of the latter be for purposes of amusement or of commerce. I need hardly say, that the doctrine of contagion still holding its ground in most continental countries, the *cordon sanitaire* and the quarantine are conscientiously employed to keep back the dreaded disease which, under the name of the plague, has so often chastised the inhabitants of large cities, in proportion to their adherence to the traditions of filth. The Quarantine at Odessa is one of the best. The buildings appropriated to the purpose skirt one of the two divisions of the harbour. In one of these divisions lie the detained vessels, and double walls and numerous sentinels effectually guard the crews from access to the town. A watch tower, situated on the pier, commands a perfect view of every part of the harbour, and is chiefly employed in the winter, when, from the presence of ice, communication with the shore is naturally easier. In the summer, I am informed, the sentinels parade with empty muskets, but in the winter they load, in order to put the shortest and sternest termination to any breach of quarantine on the part either of the men, or of any of the numberless dogs who run about, hungry and masterless, in Odessa, and whose incessant differences perpetually fill the streets with howlings. The vessels being ordered into quarantine, it is in the election of the captains and others to spend the four days' term (to which the old term of twenty-one days is now reduced) in the harbour or in the building provided for the purpose. The majority choose the former, and indeed remain in the harbour during their stay in Odessa. For not only have they thus their crews under their hand, and removed from all the temptations of a large town, but the arrangement of which I am about to speak renders the transaction of business perfectly easy. At some considerable distance from the land entrance to the quarantine, and of course between the cliffs and the water, is a large enclosure, something like a decayed public garden. Certain stunted unhappy-looking trees testify to the way in which the intentions of those who laid the place out have been frustrated by the drought and heat, and the latter is also exemplified by the cracked and melted condition of the asphalte, with which it has been attempted to pave the place. Along one side and one end of this enclosure are a series of compartments through which you see the water of the harbour, but which are furnished, first with a close row of wooden bars, and secondly, at some distance beyond them, with a wire network. On the land side the effect of the arrangement is that of some of the dens in the Zoological Gardens, an effect increased by a species of narrow piazza in front of the compartments, which slightly screens a person, standing close to the bars, from the weather. On the water side these compartments are open, and look like places for bathers. The captains and seamen walk up and down on a slice of the quay behind these boxes, and from about half-past ten in the morning there is a strange and busy scene going on between them and the residents in Odessa. In the enclosure I noticed men of almost every nation. There was the Turk, his old and splendid national dress discarded, however, for the hybrid costume—half European, half Asiatic—in which the Faithful are now so constantly attired. There was the Jew, in a much more characteristic dress—the long black robe and black cap—looking like *Shylock*, and, unless his "fellow Christians" do him injustice, supporting the character in every way. There were round-faced, smiling Germans, with sandy mustaches, and red-bowled pipes. There were Italians with whiskers as black as night, and skins as sallow as unjaundiced humanity can show—they were rolling out their sonorous vowels with great emphasis—Italian, by the way, more or less pure, is the language of business here. There were Greeks in plenty—they are strong here—and one of them was pointed out to me at the opera as the richest man in Odessa. A few Frenchmen, and a few more Englishmen, contrasting by their scrupulous neatness with the careless or sordid garb of the majority of those around them, and a number of Russians, clean, closely shaved, and buttoned to the chin with almost military rigour, nearly complete the picture within the enclosure. A few women, of the lower class, were squatting about the columns of the little piazza, and occasionally exchanging shouts with some friend in quarantine—while some soldiers, on and off duty, paraded as sentinels, or lounged as idlers, and the occasional rattle of their muskets added to the impression of restraint and imprisonment.

Almost all the inhabitants of the Continent delight in making a noise, and excite the smile of the Englishman by the blatant and enthusiastic way in which they transact the smallest affair. Consequently the system of intercourse necessitated by the quarantine may not be so disagreeable to the majority of those concerned in it as it is to the low-voiced, dispassionate Anglo-Saxon. But for a gentleman, in the dress and with the manners of one of our own opulent merchants, to be compelled to thrust his face between the bars of the quarantine den, and thence to discuss mercantile matters at the top of his voice—and to repeat his remarks over and over again, while a group of foreigners, of more or less uncleanliness, are crowding upon him, shouting out their own more powerful eloquence, and saturating him with evil odours, of which that of thick tobacco smoke is the best—must be somewhat opposed to our notions of the pleasant way of doing business. But this is the process. The merchants walk about in the enclosure, and the captains and others on the quay, until the right parties catch sight of one another, and then begins the conference, *ore rotundo*, and Jews and others creep up to listen, and gain a hint rarely thrown away. " Knaves learn their business at Pera, and come to Odessa to practise it," is a saying of some acceptation here. The conferences continue for about three hours, during which time all the dialects of Europe have been filtered through that wire network—bad Italian forming the chief element in the discord. As I passed one of the compartments, the Babel was varied by the sound of several undeniable expletives, which brought me suddenly up to the bars, and I found the jolly faces of three or four English sailors beaming up among a group of black-eyed Italians, and hungry-looking Russians. They were stating some petty grievance to an English gentleman, who was good-naturedly promising to arrange it for them—their petition was what I believe a Chancery lawyer would call, " strongly supported by affidavit."

The captains in quarantine are supplied with stores at a government tariff. The supply is contracted for with the residents in the town. Arising out of the arrangement is one of the oddest unions of which I ever heard. There was, in the earlier days of Odessa (itself a town of not much more than half a century old), a rule that the contract, which was for six years, should not upon its expiration be again granted to the same person. But in the days when the quarantine was exceedingly long, the contract was so profitable that every variety of means was employed to gain it, especially as provisions were so cheap that the contractor might easily make a hundred per cent. profit, and yet satisfy his captains that they were obtaining the article 100 per cent. under the price elsewhere. A house, very desirous of continuing the contract to itself, hit upon an ingenious mode of obtaining it. There is (as I mentioned) an Opera-house here, which, despite the Russian love of music, has always been a losing concern. The firm in question volunteered, if the contract should be given to them, to take the Opera-house also, and keep it open. This was accepted, and although there was still a heavy loss by Rossini and Bellini, it was more than made up by beef and biscuits. Since that time the government, availing itself of the precedent, has made the contract and the Opera-house go together; and, although the reduced value of the former has made the latter a more serious consideration, I believe the contractors are still willing to lump the meat and music. There is another drawback upon the opera part of the contract, for there is a Russian company, whom nobody goes to see except vulgar people who cling to the extinct tradition of a national drama; and the manager of the Opera-house is compelled to leave that company his stage on the three best nights in the week (Sunday being one), and to allow them the use of his wardrobe and orchestra *gratis*.

In the corruption which prevails in all the public departments of Russia, and from the suspicion of which no public man—except the noble born and wealthy individuals who fill the very highest places, and whose characters are above all doubt—is exempt, is another of the most serious drawbacks in the way of the quarantine contractor. Bribery is absolutely essential, if business is to be done at all. It can, indeed, hardly be called bribery, it is so patent and systematic. Not a functionary who has the power of helping, or, which is more important, of hindering, but must feel the "silver rubles" in his palm. Down to the soldier who guards the quarantine yard, there is not one official whom it is not more than expedient to touch with the metallic test. And when the immense body of *employés*, which a false and mischievous system has taught to grow into a *caste* in Russia (a *caste* whose baleful agency is opposed to every step in the way of progress), is considered, it may easily be imagined how the price of keeping this swarm of petty functionaries in working temper, must, to use a homely English proverb, "take the gold off the gingerbread." But in spite of all, the right to supply, annually, a fleet varying from 800 to 1200 ships, will enable its holders to bear a good deal of the pressure from without.

CHAPTER III.

THE connection of the town of Odessa with the agriculture of Russia is, as I have intimated, that of a mouthpiece or trough. The districts whence its supplies of wheat are drawn are situate from 150 to 250 miles from this port, and the existence of the Steppe seems to preclude the possibility of cultivation, to any appreciable extent, being ever carried on within 100 miles of the town. Its population is engaged in pursuits either entirely disconnected with agriculture, or only so far connected with it as regards the ordinary dealings with grain when it has become a mere article of commerce. Its granaries form the most prominent objects in a survey of the town, and they are remarkable not only for their size, but for the architectural display lavished upon buildings which in England are usually found of the simplest and plainest character. Some of the Odessa granaries are actually erected in a style of external taste which leads the stranger at a little distance to suppose them some kind of club-house, or museum. This, however, is but one of the many evidences afforded by Odessa of the innate desire of the Russian for every kind of display.

The wheat, which is chiefly derived from the Polish provinces, is brought to Odessa in small waggons of the rudest and most primitive construction. These are drawn by a couple of oxen, and they contain eight sacks of wheat, or about three quarters and two bushels. During the chief exportation months these waggons come pouring into Odessa by hundreds *per diem.* Their contents are conveyed to the granaries, whence the wheat is afterwards transported in open carts to the port for shipment. The scene passing under the window at which I write, is as busy a one as can be conceived. A continuous stream of these carts, loaded with the grain, in sacks, has been flowing for hours down the steep and dusty streets, and slowly winding round to the narrow strip of quay whence the wheat is discharged—while the emptied carts, incessantly returning in the opposite direction, complete the circuit, which gives the spectator the idea of an endless rope in mechanical motion.

The two kinds of wheat of which the export trade of Odessa chiefly consists, are known as the *kubanka*, or hard wheat, and the *azemaia*, or soft wheat. It is this latter which is in demand in England, the former being of a flinty, glassy grain, and chiefly required in the ports of the Mediterranean, or the south of France, and Italy. It is used for macaroni, vermicelli, and other compositions of a similar kind. The soft wheat is both white and red, but the latter is chiefly demanded for exportation. It should weigh, when of the best quality, from 61lbs. to 62lbs. per old Winchester bushel, and when of second quality, about 56lbs.

Odessa is, however, supplied with wheat from other sources, although not to any thing like the quantity furnished from the provinces of Poland; under which title is included, in general parlance, the province of Podolia, formerly a part of Poland, and from 250 to 340 miles from the port. The Danube supplies Odessa with wheat which is produced in Wallachia and in Moldavia. This wheat is brought in open vessels, exposed to a dangerous voyage, and frequently arrives in a damaged condition from the wet to which it has been subjected. There is also wheat from Cherson, and from the provinces north of it, which is furnished to the port here. But the whole of these supplies are small in comparison with what is brought by the waggon-transit.

The trade is chiefly in the hands of merchants in Odessa, or resident in other cities; but it is shared by individuals who own vessels and engage in the traffic " by way of earning a certain freight, with a hope of profit on the speculation."

The question of roads, and the general transit system of a district, is necessarily one of the earliest subjects to which attention is directed in estimating the capabilities of a country. We have just seen what exports are conducted into the Black

Sea by way of Odessa. In order to judge at what cost the most important of those exports is thus brought, and in order to enable an inquirer to predict with any approach to certainty what could be done under the pressure of the most extraordinary temptation from without, let us leave the sharp stones, deep mud, or clouds of dust of Odessa, and examine the tracks along which those long lines of bullock waggons come creaking from more northerly directions. I have said that a vast belt of Steppe girdles this coast. We are upon the Steppe. The prevailing colour, as far as the eye can reach over the immense plain, is a scorched brown. The intense heat and drought have reduced the Steppe to this condition, and far beyond the horizon line, and away, verst upon verst, is the same dreary-looking and apparently waste expanse. Not that it is all flat—hills, barren and rugged, diversify the line, and add to its difficulties in dry weather considerably, in wet incalculably. For look at the ground on which you stand. You are on one of the roads, as they are termed. Elsewhere, a road, good or bad, means something which has been *made*—a line upon which has been gathered material for binding and clasping, and below which there is some kind of draining; bad or good, the road is, as compared with the adjacent land, dry, compact, and elastic. Dismiss all such ideas from your mind, or rather drag your limbs for an hour behind that corn waggon, and such ideas will disappear of themselves. Dead and helpless seems that wobegone track, creaking and drawling over which comes the bullock waggon—all wood, and built precisely as waggons were built a thousand years ago. The driver sits in front, occasionally lashing the grey bullocks, more by way of form than with any idea of hastening them, and his massy beard hangs down over a species of censer, whence arise fumes of an unsavoury kind. But it is not in luxury, or in imitation of his eastern neighbours, that the peasant keeps this odour-breathing vessel under his nose—the contents are an abominable mixture for greasing the wheels of his waggon, and by which you may track it through many a yard of tainted air. Why he has placed the reeking vessel exactly between his legs I know not, unless it be to remind himself more forcibly of the necessity of an operation, without the incessant performance of which his clumsily built cart would be on fire in four places at once. Contrast this wretched machine with the well-contrived, iron-mounted cart of the German colonist, a few miles hence. But on goes the waggoner, jolting and creaking along the unhelpful soil, and singing some of those old airs in which, rude as they are, there is a certain melody, or saying prayers to cne or other of the multifarious national saints. On he goes, and so he and his predecessors have gone since corn was grown in Russia. Rickety cart, knotted rope harness, drowsy bullocks, wretched road—so crawls the loaf towards the Englishman's table.

We stand on the Steppe in dry weather. Weary as is the march, it is still feasible. But should rains descend, the transit becomes one of the most painful difficulty. The track is a marsh, and the feet of the hills are quagmires. The ill built waggons groan and toil against the obstructive mud, and occasionally lose their wheels in the soil. Still, the pertinacious Russian holds on; he prays, but he works too—*orat et laborat*—and somehow or other the cart is brought into Odessa, nothing lost except time, which in Russia is nothing. The average rate at which these waggons travel, under the most favourable circumstances, is about ten miles a day; and as the nearest point at which any thing like agriculture commences is considerably beyond one hundred, it is hardly necessary for me to dilate upon the advantages of the transit system as at present conducted. Were we theorizing on the question of increased demand and supply of food, it would be necessary to inquire what possible price could repay the transmission of wheat from any greater distances than those from which it is now sent by the means I have described.

To facilitate this consideration, we may place the price of land carriage of wheat as follows. For a distance of about two hundred miles, which may be taken as the average distance from which the wheat is brought (I will hereafter indicate the precise places, when upon the agricultural portion of the subject), it is conveyed for one silver ruble and a half per chetwert. The price has risen to two rubles and a half, but the above is the present rate. The price of such conveyance has risen considerably since any official inquiry upon the point was made for England; and the causes which are assigned for such increase, are the frightful mortality which has of late been manifested among the cattle, the increased difficulty in the way of obtaining pasturage upon the Steppe, and the confiscation, since 1832, of so many of the estates which belonged to various Polish nobles, and which lay along the line of travel.

There are two principal seasons of transit, namely, from the beginning of June, for about six weeks, and again towards September, after the respective harvest times. At the time I write, the second of these seasons is drawing to a close. Our own performances of the last ten years naturally set an Englishman's head running upon boilers and sleepers, the moment he hears of a difficulty of transit. A railway from Odessa into the heart of the corn-producing provinces is, of course, the first thing which will occur to him after reading what has been written. Before I conclude, I shall be enabled, I think, to supply data which will enable him to form an opinion whether, if such a railway could be suddenly flung down by miracle across the Steppe, as a drawbridge in old times fell across a castle moat, it would cause an important alteration in the wheat traffic. But one thing is tolerably certain—namely, that without such a miracle, there is wonderfully little chance of the railway. In all this monster empire, while the rest of Europe has been spinning its myriads of iron cobwebs from wall to wall, and from tower to tower, one line has been laid down (I do not speak of Poland), and that one a line which was all but unnecessary, and which actually runs along one of the few lines of Russian intercourse for which a capital road had already been laid down. The undertaking was either a job, or a mere effort of vanity; probably both. But it will not be imitated. Railroads are not encouraged in Russia; they are considered as connected in some way with the revolutionary tendencies of the age, and are accordingly disfavoured. As regards the transit of soldiery—the only point, of course, upon which it is worth the while of Russian authority to consider them—the matter has been pondered, and the Emperor finds that he can move his armies (their appurtenances taken into account) as advantageously without rails as with them. As to private enterprise here, that is entirely out of the question. Without pausing to ask whether you can expect railway progress in a country which leaves one of its most splendid and important ports undrained and unlighted, or where the nation's very almanac is left a laughing-stock to Europe, we shall find that a more practical, if not a more real, obstacle opposes itself to the establishment of railways were they ever so much desired. *There is no capital.* The sinews of railway war are wanting. The money could not be found. In saying this, I am simply recording the answer made by tradesmen, by merchants, by proprietors, by natives, as well as foreigners, and even (in whispers) by daring officials, when questioned concerning the stagnation of all national and popular enterprise—" We have no money as a nation." I have received this answer a hundred times. Many Russians are rich, but Russia is poor. With this answer, of course, ceases my share in the question, as it appears to meet the inquiry which would occur to an Englishman on first considering the position of Odessa.

But while speaking of roads, I may as well make a reference which will save a digression hereafter. The road system throughout Russia is as bad as can well be conceived. This statement will receive little favour from the wealthy traveller whose carriage has rushed almost at railway speed along the road from Moscow to the capital; but it will be confirmed by those who do not rest upon an exceptional case, and who are acquainted with the real interior of the country. No repair is ever done in Russia until it is demanded by ruin. The "stitch in time" is a species of salvation held unorthodox by the Russian. When mortar falls out, or stucco peels off, he waits until the wall totters, or the house front is a mass of blisters, before taking any step in the matter. A crack in the roof is not worth attending to; but when the rain has descended for a few weeks, and a few strata of ceilings are destroyed, and the ground floor is getting rotten, he begins to think something ought to be done. So with the roads. The hole, which a few kopecks would have set right, is left until it becomes a chasm, and then fills with water. The broken or dislodged stone is neglected until it becomes an agent in breaking and dislodging other stones, and the passage is rendered dangerous. Finally, a great man is fortunately thrown out of his vehicle by the obstruction—or, better still, a little great man, because he will make ten times as much fuss about the injury as an important personage, and there is the more chance of action. The road is then repaired, but how? Take as an instance the case of a Royal progress in Russia.

We know with what sincerity and earnestness our own population—whether its business be weaving silk or ploughing soil, raising coals or turning cheeses, dyeing broad cloth or sowing broadcast—rushes, shouting, to line the road along which our own Sovereign passes on one of her tours. There is no factitious pleasure in the sturdy cheering and shriller hurrahs with which the male and female peasantry of England receive the Queen as her carriage glides through their ranks. We have no right to suppose that the Russians, when they cheer their Emperor, are less sincere. On the contrary, it is considered that the principle of personal devotion to the Czar is remarkably powerful. But it is the Emperor's pleasure, though he has no railways, to travel at a speed which, upon that point, leaves the railway little to boast of. The tremendous pace of the Imperial carriage is proverbial. Horses in Russia all go very fast, but the Emperor's horses fly. To render such travelling practicable, the road must be looked to. The orders are given, the *corvée* is enforced, serfs are hurried up from the greatest distances, and at the times most injurious to their interests, and they work night and day. The road is patched, sand is thrown over it, and it looks remarkably neat—all that has been wanted, is that it shall be able to bear the passage of a couple of flying carriages. All—for from the time the progress is known the road is barricaded—the ordinary passengers must turn aside to another road, if there be one; at all events, the road must be kept inviolate. The day comes, and so does the Emperor—a cry of serfs, a cloud of dust, and the Sovereign is there, behind a group of maddened horses, tearing

over the ground like the ruck at the Derby, just before the
"stars" finally break away for the struggle. Something like the
same scene is witnessed after the race, for the public may now
rush upon the ground, and the road may take care of itself until
wanted again for a similar purpose.

A French engineer was recently expressing at Moscow his
decided contempt for the Russian system in reference to public
works. "If they do attempt any thing decent," he said, "they
never quite finish it, far less keep it in order. When I travel,
if I feel my carriage suddenly descend into some dreadful hole,
and I am shaken into all corners of it at once, as we struggle
out, I only remark, 'Ah, another specimen of Russian art!'"

Eminently agricultural as is Russia as a country, there are
several phases of her peasant life which it would not be accurate
to class among the manifestations of her agricultural system, and
which yet have so strange a connection with it, that they cannot
be passed over in an agricultural survey. And inasmuch as, from
the nature of these, they force themselves upon the attention of
a stranger before he has completed his examination of the system upon which they are excrescences, it may not be amiss to
dispose of them in the same order. Let us therefore give a
sketch of the position of the peasant who goes into a species of
exile, which sometimes ultimately becomes, practically, a real
banishment.

We have to contemplate a working man under an aspect, to
appreciate which we must set aside all preconceived notions of
the condition of the poor. We have to examine the pursuits,
prospects, and habits of a man who is not, except in the most
limited sense, a free agent. We have not to speak of him who,
elbowed from his place by competition, ground down by penury,
or encumbered by a craving family, is willing to give his labour
for the lowest, or any amount of remuneration which will keep
him and his children from actual starvation—but we have to
speak of him who is the lawful and recognized property of
another man, and whose intellect, strength, and skill, like his
bones and muscles, absolutely belong to his possessor and master. We have to look at the serf. Into the inherent character

of the serf system in Russia, it would be foreign to my purpose to go. This monster institution (I cannot be said to misuse the name, when I remember that out of the 54,000,000 of whom the Russian population is understood to be composed, 42,000,000 are serfs, and but 12,000,000 free—about one in five) has been for years one of the objects upon which the pens of European economists have been exercised. Its vices are known to the world; nor have those interested in preserving it failed to set forth its alleged alleviations. The opinions, too, which the respective rulers of Russia have entertained upon it are also on record. It is even no secret, that the earlier convictions of the present Emperor of Russia (whose political education was confided to abler hands than usually direct the studies of Continental royalty) were in favour of modifying the system, and elevating, if not of enfranchising the millions. Nor is it concealed, among the few who dare speak at all, that the Czar's feelings upon the subject of serfdom did not exhaust themselves in mere words, and that his Majesty actually assumed the initiative in a course which would have led to serf-emancipation. It is considered in certain circles the reverse of a matter for regret, that resolute and implacable opposition, manifested not in overt act, but in dogged and dead-weight inaction, succeeded in causing the discomfiture and abandonment of the attempts in question. Nor is it probable that such attempts will be renewed from the same quarter. The Emperor's chief attention is now given to the soldierly education of myriads of plumed and glittering serfs of his own. A taste for military detail and display has succeeded, at Petersburgh, to any effort for the settlement of graver questions, and, for the present, serfdom in Russia must remain what it is. The difficulty of any interference with it is still further enhanced by the example to which its defenders have been enabled to point, through the unparalleled ferocity and barbarity of certain serfs who (it was said, under some misconception of the pleasure of the Emperor himself) set to work to emancipate themselves. The atrocities they committed—which caused them to be hunted down like wild beasts—are pointed to as warnings how you entrust with liberty men who are not suited

for it. Murders, violations, mutilations, of the most horrible
kind, were among the first sacrifices of these men at the altar of
freedom, and are a powerful, if not an altogether silencing argument in the mouths of those who would keep barred the gates of
the temple.

Very far, indeed, is it from my intention to indulge in any
apologies for the system. An Englishman can have but one
feeling as to the position of a man on a social level with the
horse he flogs. But it is not so very long since a similar state
of things existed in our own colonies; and let us therefore quietly
examine the working of the system, leaving the reader to insti-
tute his own comparisons and deduce his own conclusions.

I have spoken of a certain species of serf as an exile, and I
propose to glance at his position before referring to that of his
resident brothers in bondage. It is this. The serf of a proprietor who resides, perhaps, several hundred miles from a certain
large town, conceives that he shall "better himself" by leaving
his native soil and trying his fortune in the town in question.
He is a carpenter, or a mason, or has a general knowledge of
some trade, though he may be engaged in agricultural pursuits.
He proposes to his lord to let him go. Possibly his lord refuses,
and there is an end of the matter; for the special case of the
serf's taking leave without permission—in other words, escaping
—is not now very frequent. Some time since, when government was desirous that the population of certain districts should
be increased, the system of running away, on the part of serfs,
and hiding in those districts (where ultimately they became
"inscribed") was winked at; but I believe the case is now
different, and that, unless the serf is almost miraculously lucky
in evading all the network of the police system, he is unceremoniously seized, packed off to the military depôt, made a
soldier, and "accounted for" to his owner, when the latter has
to pay his next instalment of serfs to the military authorities.
But if the serf have a humane and liberal owner (and I am informed that there are hundreds of such), who can afford to part
with him, the adventurer departs. He previously makes his
bargain with his owner, as to how much of his earnings shall be

remitted to the latter, and the necessary passports from his proprietor are furnished to the police of the district in which he
proposes to settle. The police system is so diffused, and has
such manifold ramifications, that it is almost impossible to evade
it long, and hence the owner has a safe hold upon the travelling
serf even at the distance of five, six, or seven hundred miles; for
nobody is allowed to live in Russia without leave, that is, without a *billet de séjour*, which has to be renewed every year—but
in the case of the serf, and indeed of others, as the police may
see fit, at the expiration of a much shorter period. In the serf's
case, I believe, six months is usually the time. If the man has
his lawful *billet*, which is strictly local, it is evidence that he has
not run away; if he has it not, he is liable to be instantly seized.
I am supposing, however, that he proposes to keep faith. He
obtains his police *billet*, and he then seeks for what work he can
get. Often, indeed most frequently, he does not leave his native
place, except in company with a "gang" of companions similarly
situated, who engage themselves *en masse*, under an arrangement
to which all must be parties, and who have a leader, who conducts the business for them, and receives and divides their
earnings. In this case they usually live together, and you meet
them returning at night, in a body, to the large room in which
they sleep, and in which they always indulge the Russian habit
of eternal singing, to the no small dissatisfaction of involuntary
audiences of neighbours.

The serf remains, and works. His rate or wages, of course
varies with his trade and with his skill. A carpenter's wages
will, for instance, vary from two rubles copper (about 1s. 10d.)
to one ruble silver a day (3s. 4d.), or he may be so excellent a
workman as to be hired, by contract, for forty-five rubles per
month. He has to pay his lodging, and he has to remit his payments to his lord. And, if he have left a wife behind, and his
inclination be to assist her efforts at self-support, he has the same
means of remitting to her, namely, by the post-office—a very
important department of which is appropriated to this kind of
business. The rest of his earnings he may apply as he pleases.

The bare necessaries of life are remarkably cheap in Russia.

The workman's living costs him the merest trifle. Vegetables, constitute its chief article, although beef, which is excellent here, is but a penny per pound. But the lower class in Russia eat little meat, and prefer all kinds of mixtures, into some of which, however, meat is admitted. A species of soup, which they call *borsh*, and which has a sour-krout feature strongly developed, is one of their great viands. There is another preparation (which I thought on tasting far less objectionable) which is made of barley, ground with the shells. Immense melons—which, as I mentioned in an earlier chapter, are here in great profusion, at a nominal price, but which are very deficient in what we consider flavour—are much in vogue with the labourer, who will cheerfully make his dinner off some hunches of melon, some black bread, and some bad water. But all kinds of vegetables are in favour, especially cabbages, which I am informed will be seen in vast numbers, in the bazaar, in a short time, and whose coming constitutes an important era in the *cuisine* of the poor. To tea, however, the Russian of all classes is vastly addicted, and I have seen more tea made since I arrived here than I have seen for years together in England. Much of it is brought overland from China, and is called caravan tea— and a good deal comes from England. The tea-urn in Russian dwelling-houses, with its fire secreted under it, is a prominent object, and the usual vessel in which you take the liquid is a tumbler, except where innovation has spread. The labourer is choice in his tea, and would probably hint to the landlord—illustrating his subject by most uncompromising references to alleged indiscretions on the part of all the latter's female relatives— that he had mistaken his vocation, were the water as much smoked as I have known it to be, with impunity, in very genteel circles in England. There is another fluid, called *quass*, which is made of water into which bread is thrown and allowed to ferment, of which the labourer is also very fond, but I have not gone further than looking at this unspeakable nectar.

The labourer respects his *Voskrisinie*—that is, to a certain extent. If you particularly wish him to work on the Sunday, he will, of course for a consideration. But there is a series of days upon which no earthly power, unless that of the Emperor himself, who can hardly be called a mere earthly power in Russia, could induce him to labour. These are the days which are set apart to the saints. These days are always coming, and they bring with them idleness and debauchery. No matter how important it may be to get a certain work done, the Russian will not give up the observance of a saint's day upon any compulsion. He dresses himself with an attention to his toilet which is by no means his failing—washes his hands, and, I believe I am right in adding, his face—puts on a clean outside shirt, tucks his trousers into his boots (a very sensible practice, by the way, and one which might be considered in countries where people protect half a yard of leather by covering it with fine cloth, reversing the obvious arrangement) and goes to church. In the afternoon, of course, he gets very drunk. Any attempt to reform this system would be pretty sure to produce a rebellion.

The institution of tea-houses has had a beneficial effect upon the Russian workman. There are many of these places in Odessa; the prices are very low, and they have materially injured the cellars where spirituous liquors (especially *votki*) are sold. Still, however, there are numbers of the latter, and on the Sundays and saint-days the Russian labourer reels from them in a state of almost entire stupefaction; the usual object, I should observe, in drinking—the jovialty and enjoyment of social intercourse, which form the bad and only extenuation for excess—having little place in his character. He would concur with an old officer in our army, who, hearing certain port wine found fault with, conceived that he could defend it in one comprehensive plea—" I don't see what you can say against this wine, gentlemen—I really don't. It's black, and it's thick, and it makes one drunk."

It is due, however, to the Russian workman to add, that he adheres rigidly to the fasts of his Church; and, although his habitual use of vegetable diet may render this more easy to him than it would be to a flesh-eater, he deserves all the credit which such observances may demand. Some of the labourers, I am informed, carry their scrupulosity to such a point, that upon the fast-day they will not even sweeten their tea with sugar, because, although that is a vegetable substance, blood is used in refining it. These extra punctilious devotees, therefore, keep a raisin in their mouths, to supply the necessary sweetening.

It should be mentioned, also, that certain provinces acquire a reputation for furnishing expert artificers in particular trades, and that the natives of such provinces are somewhat more acceptable in the large towns of Russia than are persons from other departments. And this does not alone depend, as might naturally be imagined, upon the class of occupation to which the province in question seems likely to give encouragement or especial scope. Supposing that we were compelled to ransack the English counties for stone-cutters or smiths, we should feel as great difficulty in deciding where to look for either, but the Russian would not proceed upon precisely the same calculation. It is customary with the proprietors of serfs to select promising youths, whom they apprentice to such trades as they may consider most likely to turn out profitably to themselves. The youth is sent to some busy place to acquire instruction in his calling, and this added skill has, of course, corresponding advantage for the owner of the trained workman. And their various districts have gained what is probably a shifting reputation, as the *depôts* for good masons or carpenters. Nor are the men themselves insensible to the vanity of claiming connection with a province in repute. Several of the workmen with whom I have spoken referred, in a knowing way, to the spots whence they had come, and which I found enjoyed this species of reputation! I am informed, however, that the apprenticeship system is by no means invariably successful. The young serf comes to a busy place, learns his trade—perhaps among free workmen, or at all events where he has the opportunity of seeing such men—finds that he can soon work as well as they can, but that he is working for another, who makes a large harvest out of his earnings. He sees no chance of improving the condition whose hardship he has been taught to discover, and he becomes sullen, discontented, and a drunkard.

The return of the adventurous serf is very uncertain. Sometimes he saves sufficient money to enable him to retire from the town, and go home; and then, if he can obtain his passports, all is well. But the police system bears very hard upon these men, and the lower class of proprietors are known to avail themselves of it for the meanest oppression. Instances have been known in which, after the lord has fixed the price of his serf's freedom, and the unfortunate fellow has transmitted the earnings of years to purchase the documents necessary for the manumission, the lord has neglected to furnish such documents, and the wretched serf's applications have been in vain, until he has been obliged to return to his toil, wearied out and heart-broken, and any inquiry on the part of a pitying superior has been met by the ready falsehoods of instructed subordinates. I have been furnished with some remarkable stories of this kind, which disclose a baseness that is, one would hope, of rare occurrence. But supposing the serf meets honourable treatment, and the exactions of the police are all complied with, he can purchase himself into a condition which we will consider hereafter.

CHAPTER IV.

THE Russian territory bordering on the Black Sea may, as regards the purpose of our inquiry, be described under the following titles:—Bessarabia, Podolia, Kherson, Kiev, and Tauride. Although the limits of two of the most important of the provinces I have mentioned do not approach within a great distance of the sea (I mean Podolia and Kiev), both are so inseparably connected with the agriculture of Southern Russia, and with the harbour of Odessa, that it would be impossible to exclude them from our inquiry; the more so that the agricultural system of Russia is more largely developed, both as regards its advantages and its defects, in those two provinces, than in those more closely bordering the Euxine. For the province of the Steppe, lying in a broad brown band between the green fields and the blue waters, effectually deprives the lower provinces of a vast share of agricultural importance. Indeed, as regards the Crimea (Tauride), its agricultural produce is and must be comparatively trifling, being raised only for the support of its own population, and, as regards the far larger part of the locality, wrung from Steppe land. But while this latter portion of the territory of the empire will demand but an unimportant place in our inquiry, the vast and rich provinces lying more to the north—whence really proceeds the grain-wealth of the south of Russia, and where must be sought the battle-ground between the advocates of two systems—will require an examination of a somewhat extended character.

It may be necessary for me here to apologize, or rather to account, for my entering into a larger detail, in connection with various topics arising out of the survey before me, than may at first sight appear absolutely necessary. Certain parts of this

detail may not at once be seen to assume their place in reference
to my general object. But I venture to hope that it will ultimately be seen, that I have recorded little which is not useful
towards a general comprehension of the subject. In reality, the
task of rejection is by far the most troublesome one to an inquirer who has other objects in view than filling his sheet with
novel and characteristic sketches, or with that pleasant and in-
forming gossip for which ordinary readers are so justly grateful.
It will also be remembered that the majority of Englishmen
know far less of the interior of Russia, and even of the general
social system of that country, than they do of India or America,
and that the very Guilds of the empire are institutions little
known to thousands who are familiar with the fact, that

> " The Brahmins in the fields of day,
> The harmless amulet of Castes display."

In very briefly recapitulating, therefore, the principal features
of the Russian system, I may be allowed to consider that I am
dealing with the data upon which the personal and industrial
freedom of the population of the country must be discussed, as
well as the alleged existence of laws and customs prejudicial to
commerce and industry. And as regards such subordinate
details as, at the apparent risk of digression, may be introduced,
I will merely ask indulgence until it shall be seen whether they
have assisted in affording the desired insight into the practical
working of the systems under investigation.

"*Apis, anser, vitulus,*" says an old writer (alluding, I need
hardly say, to the goose-quill, the parchment, and the seal)
"govern this world." Freely translating the zoological triad
into "pen, ink, and paper," I may truly state that a similar
holy alliance governs Russia. In this country a man is nothing; his obvious flesh and suggested bones are nothing;
he is unrecognised; he is unseen; in fact, he is invisible (with
an exception in favour of certain microscopic observers in uniform), unless he has in his possession a certain piece of paper.
Whether he be a stranger or one born in the land, the rule is
the same. It applies equally to the Russian Ivan Ivanovitch,
servant at my hotel, and at present making my bed with a cigar

in his mouth—to the Greek merchant who has just passed my window, and is the richest man in Odessa—and to myself. To be a Russian, or to live in Russia, you must be inscribed in the books of the police, and, in proof that you are so inscribed, you must have a species of ticket, *billet*, passport, or call it what you please. And this ticket you must renew every year. And you must be prepared to produce it whenever thereunto invited by any thing wearing the uniform of the Emperor's servants. Without this ticket you are nobody ; your rights are untenable, your privileges are neutralised; and, no matter how rich, how noble, how learned, how virtuous you are, without this you are in a position of doubt and suspicion, which, if you allow it to endure, will with fatal rapidity be converted into a condition more unpleasant still. In a word, every body in Russia must have his ticket of leave to live. To enforce this great law, there is a vast army of police, spies, and others, all so deeply interested in the maintenance of the system, that there is no chance of escaping or evading it.

Now, though a national habit may easily be pronounced unwise, we must inquire before we pronounce upon its estimation among the people. One thing is certain—namely, that no member of the Greek faith can well complain of a system which may be said to form part of the articles of his belief. This is no flippancy of speech. When the battle of life is fought, and its dead soldier is brought into the house of God, that the last rites may be performed over the body, watch the process. After certain ceremonies of an imposing character, the priest approaches the coffin, which is open, and strews incense upon the breast of the dead. He then reads a paper, unfastens the front of the dress of the corpse, and places the document in the bosom. The interment then proceeds. That document is a *certificate and passport*, without which (duly *visé* by the priest) the officer in charge of the gate of heaven would refuse entrance to the soul of the departed. Even St. Peter demands the sight of a soul's papers. What word of objection can a worshipper of St. Peter make to such a system? He must, on the contrary, rather regard the renewing of his *billet de séjour* as a species of religious ceremony, and look upon the police officials as resembling his own priests—a point in which he will not greatly slander either party, both being, very generally, remarkably venal, dissolute, and worthless.

It must be remembered that there is no recognised distinction of honour in Russia, except one—distinction acquired by military service. Every man who desires to rise to dignities must make the army his ladder. Through that ascending filter must be purified all the aspiring spirits of the country. The father of his people does not know his children except in uniform. There can be no souls above buttons here. So far, the system is impartial. The child of the oldest house in Russia must ascend every step *pari passu* with the *parvenu*. Providence may have made him a count—that is nothing. Has the Emperor made him a colonel? The poorest and meanest creature who has a step in advance of him is for the present his superior, and entitled to be so treated. And this is not, be it observed, merely like the English, or any other army system. It is nothing, of course, to the Honourable Algernon St. Julians, and Lord Evelyn Trevor, that the third dandy standing in the club window with them, and helping them to scandalize the broughams, is the son of a grocer, and their superior in the army—his father's plums having told at the Horse Guards, while the St. Julians' entail and the Trevor mortgages keep the others waiting a little for their steps. Military rank, unless very high indeed, has no weight in society in England—except that, the older the officer, the more are light-minded people inclined to edge away from him, lest he should be loaded with long stories, and go off by unhappy accident. But in Russia the distinctions of military rank are every thing. The court sets the example of valuing them before all else, and of rewarding with them those whom it delights to honour. Titles sound well; but they are, indeed, but sounding brass and tinkling cymbals, unless they bear some official affinity to the brass and cymbals of a regiment. Lord Evelyn and Mr. St. Julians would find the difference between themselves and Mr. Fitzvalentia if they and the young grocer were announced at a party in Russia. The Russian world is too full of officials, each tremblingly alive to the exact limits of his position, not to maintain the inches of vantage in the strictest order. A living lieutenant here is a great deal better than the son of a dead hero, if the son's hero-worship has not taken him to drumhead altars.

But if the system affected the army only, it would be by no means so opposed as it is to an Englishman's notion of the fitness of things. If grades mean any thing, they mean obedience and command, and, if people like to keep their respective positions in sight at times when other people prefer to forget them, that is mere matter of taste. But the military system is not more than half seen when seen only in connection with the army: To say nothing of the curious anomaly of giving military rank to the naval officer—whereby one sees a gentleman in a long cloak and boots marching from paddle-box to paddle-box, and giving orders to the helmsman with the air of a warrior waving his troops to the charge—the bearing of the system on civil life is most remarkable. Although, of course, to be any thing but a soldier is beneath the dignity of human nature, still, such are our plebeian wants, that even in Russia there must be tutors, and physicians, and architects, and other inferior creatures. But if these people wish to be any thing more than contemptible beings, who teach, and cure, and build, they, too, must have recourse to the army. Military rank is necessary to elevate them into a decent sociable position, and military rank is accorded to them. A captain birches your little boy, and a major prescribes your rhubarb and magnesia, and a lieutenant designs the pediments and architraves for your grand new house. Custom-house clerks, post-office clerks, passport-office clerks, are all in uniform; and when they fill the pit of the theatre, and their manifold buttons sparkle in the light of the oil-fed chandelier, the effect, coupled with that of their stubbly heads—which, according to rule, are all cropped as closely as those of convicts—is, to say the least of it, remarkable. There are no less than fourteen different ranks in the "civil service," and each of them has a corresponding military value. Thus a *Conseiller de Cour* is a Major, a *Conseiller de Collège* is a Lieutenant-Colonel, a *Conseiller d'Etat* is a Colonel, a *Conseiller*

d'Etat Actuel is a Major-General, a *Conseiller Privé* is a Lieu-
tenant-General, and a *Conseiller Privé Actuel* is a full General.
The lowest is, I believe, the Registrar of College, whose rank is
about that of an Ensign, but whose dignified duties probably
exalt him to the office of copying letters, and similar diplomatic
exploits. Of course, all these gentlemen are in the service, but
such among them as have professional engagements combine
them with their duties to the State; and, when they retire from
the latter, they preserve the military rank, which makes Russia
resemble a vast barrack. I paid a visit with a friend, a few
mornings ago, to the house of one of these civil heroes, and, in
reply to the inquiry of my companion, the servant said, " Yes,
sir, the general is here." I had prepared myself for the sight of
a soldierly person, bearing the marks of service, and probably
clanking a variety of the orders which are showered over Russia
like the bon-bons at a child's party. I suddenly found myself
looking down upon one of the tiniest, and whitest, and most
meek of human creatures, who was bowing to my companion
with exuberant gratitude for a business favour, and looking as
if the untimely slamming of a door would scare the very soul
out of him by the shortest cut. For a general, he bore a wonderful resemblance, so far as capability of service went, to another
eminent military person of the same rank, who some time ago
took London by storm, commanding under the modest title of
Tom Thumb.

Were the effects of the system simply ridiculous, however, it
would scarcely be worth remarking on; but it has a far more
vicious tendency. The official, with his sonorous rank of Lieu-
tenant-General, or the like, contracts an unhappy habit of ex-
penditure, not in accordance with his real, but with his nominal
rank. Lavish extravagance is common to the national character;
but this system in a manner forces it upon individuals, and
it is no uncommon thing to see men whose official income does
not amount to two hundred a year, living at the rate of eight or
ten. Where the balance comes from, is of course the stranger's
question—the native answers it with a shrug. The man has an
official position, which enables him to be useful or a hindrance

to the public who have to come in contact with him. He is
compelled to seek bribes, and the public are compelled to give
them. The frightful and shameless bribery which charac-
terises official life in Russia, spreading through all ramifications
of public service, and contaminating all that should be honest
and impartial, is one of the worst features of the domestic
system, and is much increased by the foolish military classification
which I have described. But even the splendid contempt which
the real soldier here, as elsewhere, manifests for the sham one,
does not disconcert the latter, who is as proud of his livery as
possible. The actual soldier regards these imitations much in
the way that an officer in the Guards scrutinises a captain in a
Yeomanry corps, or an officer in the Artillery regards one in the
Artillery company. There is also another stall in Vanity Fair
which has large dealings here — the Order booth. To see the
mass of these appendages which hang along a species of line,
stretched across the breast of the meanest and dirtiest-looking
individual, would really scandalize one who was disposed
to see, in the careful bestowal of such honours, a wise method of
conferring honorary distinction. But to remark the kind of
persons who come down to the pier, or to quarantine, with two,
three, four, five, and more ornaments dangling and clicking on
their greasy great-coats, is what our American friends call a
" caution." I need hardly say that no such observation includes
the noble and honourable order of St. George (founded by
Catherine II.), and which may be known by its enamelled cross
of white and its escutcheon. This, in all its degrees, is an honour ;
but in its first class it implies the performance by the wearer of
one of those actions which make a reputation for all time. The
late Duke of Wellington was, I believe, the only foreigner upon
whom this sign has been conferred. Other distinctions are bestowed in handfuls. I do not exaggerate ; for upon certain State
occasions hundreds of badges are given away—there is a perfect
rain of falling stars.

Being a soldier, in any degree, the Russian has a *status*, and
a valuable one, so far as his social position is concerned. The
soldier is peculiarly favoured in his intercourse with his fellows;

he is treated with consideration when a civilian receives nothing but rudeness, and, whenever a preference can be given, the military man, of course, obtains it. You cannot move in public resorts either of pleasure or business, or go into society, without observing that the system which is so carefully tended and so rigidly maintained, has its fruits in enforcing public respect. It is not my intention to attempt examination into the military institutions of Russia, farther than as they affect its general interests, or those of the classes more immediately connected with the land; but I may remark that the system of discipline is represented to be severe in the extreme—that the precision with which details are looked to, is fractional to a point of which our own martinets have little idea—and that the slightest departure from the smallest regulation is a crime. From what I have personally observed, of the perseverance of Russian authorities in encumbering every transaction of life with the greatest possible number of formalities and ceremonies, nine-tenths of which a simple-minded man of business would reject with great contempt, I can easily imagine that the governing spirit is not likely to be relaxed in the army. But the spy system is too perfectly organized, I am informed, to make it probable that a stranger will ever hear a complaint on these points. Such a breath would indeed agitate the vast spider-web, and the ruin of the careless murmurer would be beyond a doubt. Of the life of the Russian officer I have nothing to say. But it has been my business to know something of that of the Russian private.

The levy which supplies the huge army of Russia is entirely at the will of the Emperor. But military matters are well understood by his Majesty; and there is no reason to say, as has been asserted, that the levy is wantonly or needlessly demanded by the present Sovereign. The vast needs of such an empire, as regards armed force, can scarcely be appreciated from without; especially amid the darkness in which it is the pleasure and policy of Russia to keep the other members of the European family as to what passes within her limits. The authorities at St. Petersburg know with how many myriads they have to deal, and what manner of men those myriads may be. They have, therefore, the best materials upon which to calculate the squadrons with which it may be necessary to intimidate enemies at home and abroad. And the Emperor himself has rarely been accused of any disposition to misuse his gigantic power, so far as regards his own subjects. The military necessities of Russia may, and ought in candour to be judged by her military display—the fact itself may be simply stated in a sentence. The last return informs us that the army of Russia consists of 1,200,000 men. One man in ten is an " unproductive."

The process of hero-manufacture is not, at first sight, so agreeable to the embryo hero or to the spectator as one would expect to find the early stage of an operation so desirable. The subject upon whom the experiment is to be performed, is perhaps the serf of a lord in one of the provinces I have above named— say Podolia. He is busily engaged in getting in his little harvest, or repairing his miserable cottage for the winter. The order for the levy has reached his lord. This last time it was for seven men out of every thousand—not a very formidable lottery, if lots were the order of the day; only they are not. The selection is not made in so random a way. The lord, assisted by his stewards and other servants, decides upon the hero without the aid of the goddess Chance. Naturally he would be disposed to take care that the army should not be too well served, nor would he voluntarily send away a really valuable article of property. Of course, if he dared, the maimed, and the halt, and the blind, would be provided for at the expense of the State by the means of the levy. But, as obviously, this would not do. The army is too terrible an institution to be played with—it is the Emperor's own *protégé*, and it is one of the few institutions of the country in which vigilant and swift justice is sometimes done. No recruiting on the system so admirably carried on by *Bardolph* and *Nym* at *Master Shallow's* will be tolerated here; the man who is to serve his Czar must be a man, at least. The next question is, what well-made men can best be spared, or may be most conveniently got rid of. The most honourable and humane proprietor of serfs would,

without blame, make such a selection as would clear away the
idler, the thief, the drunkard, the *mauvais sujet* of every kind,
from his estate; and no doubt such is the rule with very many
proprietors. But that this arbitrary power of getting rid of any
obnoxious individual is frightfully misused, there can be no
doubt either. The serf who has offended his owner to a degree
for which the punishment permitted to the latter offers no
adequate vengeance, or the serf who has an inconvenient claim
upon his owner, will not feel any thing like surprise—will feel
nothing but dismay—at being pointed out for the levy; and
subordinate agencies are so frequently at work in these cases,
that they are even made the subject of jests in certain quarters.
The serf has given private offence to the exacting intendant, the
extortionate steward, or to some fellow-serf who may be under
the purchased patronage of the latter. His way to glory is
marked out for him—the lord, if present, knows nothing about
him, but has nothing to oppose to the representation of his
servant. The unhappy man is dragged from his home, his wife,
his children, one half of his head is shaved from back to front,
he is riveted up in heavy chains with the gang of his comrades,
and away he is marched to the military depôt.

There is even another agency which not unfrequently sends
away an unfortunate serf to the depôt. He may have been
lucky enough, as he foolishly imagined himself, to win the heart
of some pretty serf girl, and they may have set themselves to run
the hard race of life together, their affections drawing gradually
closer, as the feelings of these vulgar people often will, from the
incessant hardships of their lot. Such things are not uncommon, I am told, among the serfs, who are very ardent in their
attachments. But the charms which pleased the serf may also
have pleased his betters. Perhaps it is the lord, perhaps it is
only the steward, or some favourite servant, who has taken a
fancy to the pretty serf-wife. He has signified his admiration.
But sometimes it occurs that the wife will not come into the
arrangement, and is proof against bribes and threats; and her
husband, though every kind of persecution may be tried to overcome his scruples, refuses to sanction the intrigue. Let him look

out when the levy comes again. I have had some touching stories of this kind given me.

With the recruit, after he is chained and shaved, I have no more to do, wishing merely to show the mode in which the liberty of one class of agricultural labourers is understood here, and how they can be and are withdrawn from the soil they till. Seven men in every thousand does not seem a very appreciable item in a country like this; but there are 42,000,000 of serfs in Russia! The warrior himself is conducted to the depôt, and there, doubtless, his education is commenced upon the most improved principles. His comforts may suffer at first; for having been accustomed to the shaggy sheepskin, the warmest-looking article in the world, and to a thick cap, he is rendered nearly bald—he has a helmet given him—and his sheepskin is taken away in favour of the apparently thinnest uniform extant. There cannot be a greater contrast than the sturdy peasant, in the comforting dress I have described, and his shivering compatriot on duty as a sentinel when one of the Black Sea breezes runs a-muck at the town. It is the peasant who looks the soldier then, as he grins good-humouredly in the teeth of the wind. I think I agree with the Rev. Mr. Gleig, that the swaggering manner, "if it does not run wild altogether," should be rather encouraged in a soldier—if he is to be formidable, he should believe himself so. But, as far as I have seen, there is very little of this in the Russian soldier—he looks very meek, and remarkably uncomfortable. In the capital, and around the great head of the army, no doubt things look differently, or travellers would not go away with such enraptured visions of glorious and gigantic guardsmen, and reviews which do every thing but realize Milton's battle of the angels. I merely mention what I see. The soldier is not well fed, but the contrary; and when he is engaged, as he often is, by private employers, to assist in heavy work, his want of physical power, compared with the exertions of the civilian by his side, is not only evident to the eye, but registered in his wages, which are usually lower than those of his companion. I do not know that there is any reason why a soldier should be able to heave a sack easily—a man

who cannot carry a load may be very useful in carrying a town;
but I know what one of our own brawny and willing guardsmen would say, if he saw the apparent calibre of these men. In
sickness, I am glad to believe that there is an intention to amend
the treatment of the soldier—a necessary movement, considering
the immense number of the Russian army at this moment in
hospital, or unable to appear on parade. There has always been
an enormous parade of care for him when sick, and the display
of the military apothecary's gilded boxes and the like, has
always been most satisfactory upon inspection, until the boxes
were opened. But it is not very long since a discovery was
made, that through the hideous peculation and jobbing prevalent
in every part of Russia, the bark which was intended by the
Emperor for the poor soldiers—a medicine almost as necessary
as air to them, considering the quality of their food—had become, it was said, oak bark, but at all events rubbish—utterly
useless, though the Czar had originally paid an enormous price
for it. And now, at this very time, it is mentioned really as a
matter of congratulation, that the influence of Prince Woronzow
(whose whole life, as continually described to me by those who
have known him best, seems to have been a constant struggle to
ameliorate the condition of all within his reach) has introduced
quinine into the medical chests of the army. What I have seen
and heard, therefore, of the condition of the Russian soldier, does
not tend to increase my faith in the system of which he is part;
but as I have been dazzled by no review, and have not even
gazed with awe upon the armed giants of St. Petersburg,
allowance must be made for the flatness of my description, when
contrasted with the *couleur de rose* statements with which be-
wildered travellers from the Neva return to bewilder their
friends.

But commercial life has its classifications in Russia as well as
military life, and the distinctions which are laid down by law
are as rigidly defined in one case as in the other—although, of
course, it is the tendency of any very arbitrary rule to defeat
itself, and, in reality, this is the result as regards many of the
regulations to which I am about to refer. The mercantile and

trading population of Russia is divided by law into several
classes, each having a different share of privileges and advantages.
The division is somewhat elaborate; but as it will be seen that it
has, and professes to have, a directing and restraining influence
upon commerce, I shall not be performing a work of supereroga-
tion in very briefly explaining it.   The mercantile world, then,
is separated by law into a series of ranks, three of which (but
not the highest) are called guilds.   The members of the highest
order are known as Notables.   To enter this class, which is
again subdivided into hereditary and non-hereditary portions, an
individual must not only be possessed of a declared capital of
50,000 rubles (paper), but must be prepared to undergo, as
regards himself and his affairs, what may be a very rigid examination, touching his habitual solvency, fulfilment of his engagements, and other observance of the rules of commercial honour.
If he enters the class of Notables, he has attained the highest
dignity to which mercantile men ever aspire, apart from official
life.   The three guilds follow.   To be inscribed as a member of the
first guild, a merchant has merely to declare a capital of 50,000
rubles.   He is then allowed to build manufactories, to have
country houses and gardens, and to carry on domestic or foreign
trade at his will.   He may also have ships; and he has another
privilege which in Russia has its own value—he may drive four
horses in his carriage.   The member of the second guild declares
to a capital of 10,000 rubles only.   He can trade within the
country, and may build manufactories, keep inns, and possess
boats; but he may drive only two horses, and I believe there is
also a condition imposed as to the character of the vehicle.   The
member of the third guild declares to a capital of 8000 rubles.
He can neither export nor import.   But he may be a retailer,
and may attend fairs and markets.   He has not the exemptions
of the first and second class, except in regard to his taxation,
which is levied, like theirs, upon the declared capital.   In other
respects he is in the same situation as the citizen class below him.
These are the inferior class of dealers, whom, though the law has
evinced much consideration for them in several respects, it has
left exposed to corporal punishment, from which the elevated

mercantile classes are exempt. Of course the restrictions upon the inferior guilds are equally binding on the citizen. Below these is a "general" class, and we then descend to serfs of the Crown, and other serfs, of whom we shall have more occasion to speak. I should add that the higher classes, including the citizens, are exempt from the conscription to which the "general" class and its inferiors are subject.

The strangers, or foreigners, are again separately classified, and upon the whole the spirit of legislation in regard to this body is liberal. They may build manufactories at pleasure, and trade as they please. And it is right to remark, that not only in regard to foreigners, but in reference to the general internal management of the affairs of the people of Russia, the spirit of the law is most liberal and wise. There is machinery provided, to a large extent, for what we term self-government by the classes most interested in its due administration. The electoral habit is that most recognised by Russian law. But it is the vicious and destroying system that has been superadded to the original institutions which has utterly ruined them, and which renders men of position and responsibility in Russia unwilling to take upon themselves—or, if elected, to concern themselves with—the duties which none could discharge better; but in the slightest effort to discharge which an independent man is met, thwarted, and crushed by the whole weight of corrupt bureaucracy. The evils of the latter system are so constantly before a traveller, that he is in danger of losing sight of the fact, that the administrative system here is, after all, but an abuse and a corruption, and that it has taken the place of a system far more akin to that of England than most persons would be inclined to believe.

Without noticing a few special class subdivisions, which do not appear to affect the questions more immediately before us, we now come to the lowest class of Russian—the serf. I have already touched upon his condition, but I have viewed him only as an inhabitant of the town. It is to the agricultural serf, in connection with the system of which he forms so important a part, that a larger share of our attention will be given. I will venture

to complete this chapter with a narrative completely bearing upon
the subject we are about to consider. It is the story of the
life, thus far, of an agricultural serf, and it was communicated
to me by a lady who possesses the best authority for the details.
The narrative struck me as at once interesting, and as illustrating several points (to be hereafter more gravely considered) in
the condition of the slave class; and although the story, told me
in French, will suffer by its being given in other than the brilliant and epigrammatic style of my accomplished acquaintance,
I do not think it will prove unacceptable.

Demetrius —— was born upon the estate of Count ——, in
Podolia—which, as I have said, is one of the most fertile of the
provinces which pour their corn upon Odessa. His mother (one
of the handsomest peasants upon the property) and his reputed
father were serfs; the former, so far as I can learn, having been a
species of village coquette in a region where coquetry has a somewhat more extended signification than among more scrupulous
people. It is right to mention this, because I have used the
words "reputed" father, and because the individual currently
supposed to have been the father, without the reputation, was a
Greek 'pope or priest of the vicinity. Certainly Demetrius,
though unable to free himself from the suspicion of being a child
of the Church, lost in after-life no opportunity of professing his
distaste for the pedigree thrust upon him. He prospered, however, under the double parentage allotted to him, and grew up,
from a favoured, active, mischievous boy, to a smart, powerful,
but dissolute and discontented young fellow. The Count, his
owner, had taken considerable notice of him, had employed him
about his horses, and had gone so far—being himself rather a
free-thinker, and wanting a sufficient awe of the traditionary
maxim in Russia against teaching slaves—as to cause the young
Demetrius to be instructed in reading and writing. But free-
thinking, especially if combined with gambling and other ex-
citing extravagances, brings no good; and when Demetrius was
about sixteen or seventeen, the Count's estates passed, if not into
other hands, under other mismanagement, and the nobleman
himself departed to reside elsewhere. The new master—who,

according to the custom of the country, became possessed of all
the authority of his predecessor—was a brutal and avaricious
man, who proposed to himself simply to extort as much as he
could from the wretched peasantry over whom his purse, which
had befriended the count in his gambler's need, had given him
sway. Things became changed—the stern rule sanctioned by
law, but which the careless, good-natured spendthrift had greatly
relaxed, was revived—and the serfs began to feel the chain
which had hitherto scarcely galled them. Of course, there was
nothing to do but to submit; for when a master has the right
to flog a man ten times a day, and to send him to Siberia upon
the mere condition of paying the expense of his transportation
thither, it hardly answers a slave's purpose to complain.

Among the earliest sufferers was the young Demetrius, who,
presuming upon his former favour, presented himself somewhat
unceremoniously to the new lord, and obeyed with such ill
grace the instant order to betake himself to field labour, that
the keen, cruel eye of his master observed his bearing. The
report of a servant of the house, who was happy to revenge
himself for some mischievous prank played him by the lad, and
rather approved by the count, was not necessary to ensure the
result. The master rode his rounds, and very speedily detected
Demetrius making some impromptu love at a time when he
ought to have been, waist deep in wet mud, repairing the side
of a dyke. A merciless flogging was administered to the young
man ; and, as soon as he was able to crawl, he betook himself to
the individual whom he was certainly entitled to believe his
father. But it was not for directions as to the road to heaven
that he proposed to consult him—a line on which the good
man's counsels might have been a little confused, especially late
in the evening. But confiding in the air of kindness in which
the shepherd usually, when conscious, addressed his sheep, Demetrius ventured to counsel him as to the road to Moscow.
And, upon a little cross-questioning, he admitted that he was
cherishing a design of escaping from the tyranny of his master,
and of finding his way to the second capital of the empire, to
seek his fortune. He had some vague idea of discovering a

F

relation of his mother's, who was said, upon the estate, to have settled and become wealthy at Moscow, and who therefore, thought the well-instructed serf, would naturally be rejoiced to see and aid an unfortunate kinsman. Nothing but the exceeding absurdity of such an idea, and the conviction that it could bring only disappointment, would have justified the priest in immediately revealing the intended attempt to the lord. The result of course was, that before Demetrius could be said to be well recovered from his first flagellation, he underwent a second, which pretty nearly deprived his savage owner of the chance of ever rendering such part of his property as was comprised in the bones and sinews of Demetrius available for the purposes nearest to his heart.

But a rather curious combination of affairs befriended him while he was lingering, almost hopelessly, under the brutal treatment to which he had been subjected. The charms of the village coquette, although that lady was now the mother of a lad of seventeen, had not entirely faded. At all events, her now full-blown attractions had sufficient power to please the coarse taste of her lord, and he—having had opportunity of fully observing her when she came to him, and upon her knees besought (vainly for the time) his forbearance towards her boy —signified his intention of taking her into favour. She became a resident in a cottage near his house, and her fascinations soon extorted from her grim lover an intimation, that if Demetrius chose to behave himself satisfactorily, he should not be again half murdered, for the present. With this charming *avenir* before him, the youth had nothing to do but to recover his health as best he might, and stifle such feelings as for the time could only interfere with his fortunes.

The influence which Anna —— gained over her master was very great, as frequently happens in the case of hard, grasping natures, which, callous and oppressive to all else around them, become plastic in the hands of some worthless favourite. Anna, however, does not seem to have exercised her power very unworthily; but, warmly attached to her son, she chiefly devoted herself to the project of purchasing his freedom from his lord.

This object was environed by a double difficulty—first, that of obtaining the necessary funds; and secondly, of becoming possessed of them in a way which would not excite the suspicion of the keen-witted tyrant himself, who, of course, well knew what chances Demetrius or his mother had of accumulating any considerable sum of money. After this observation, one need scarcely add that Anna proposed to obtain the money by simply plundering her admirer. This was no easy task, but time, vigilance, and caution enabled her to effect it; and little by little she subtracted from the hoards of her master a sum which she relied upon as sufficient for the purchase of her child's liberty. The subject had to be gradually broached, in order to avoid arousing either the suspicions or the ill feelings of the master; but Anna's position gave her many opportunities, and her woman's wit aided her. She prevailed upon her lover to promise the manumission of Demetrius, if he should ever be able to raise a sum not much exceeding that which his mother had already stolen for him; and, this point attained, she paved the way for her lord's reception of a story by which she intended to account for the possession of a portion of the purchase-money. To carry this out she required a confederate, and naturally turned in her need to one who, if scandal were not libel, was at least bound to render her all the aid in his power. She applied to the priest. Now the good man, who had begun to grow old in the practice of all the manifold rogueries of his order, had no regular access to the proprietor of the estate, the latter being a Roman Catholic, like great numbers of the lords. He promised his assistance in Anna's scheme, provided she would obtain for him certain pecuniary favours which the master, between his conscience and his cupidity, had hitherto refused to the heretic priest. The compact was struck, and a plan was arranged, materially aided by the inventive genius of the churchman, by which the latter was to be called away to a distant district, and was to return with a legacy left to Anna by a dying friend. The scheme was a good one, but all good schemes do not succeed. Anna confided her savings to her ghostly confidant, who went away with them, and there his assistance in the plot ended, for he never returned.

Robbed and deceived in her turn, Anna did not give way to despair. She had determined that her son should be free. While casting about for a new plan of action, she continued to secrete money, little by little, belonging to her master, over whom her influence increased with his advancing years. Eventually, by dint of continued entreaty, she contrived to extort from her lover his signature to a document which manumitted Demetrius —but which, as the former stipulated, should remain in his custody until the ransom money, now fixed at a far more moderate price than before, should be paid. The proprietor of Demetrius affixed the signature with seeming reluctance. But such manifestation was mere pretence. He had received from the very hands of Anna, a few days before, a letter which revealed to him the previous portion of the plan. This letter was from the Greek priest, and whether written in mere malice, or whether from that feeling which begrudges to a rival the regards of a woman even for whom one has ceased to entertain a regard, it were difficult to say. Had Anna known or guessed at the handwriting—but, unhappily, Anna could not read.

Demetrius, being made aware of the existence of the document signed by his owner, proposed to make short work of the rest. But as any step such as was contemplated by the young man would of course have destroyed Anna's position, he was compelled to remain passive until her plot could be worked out. It might have been easy for Anna to steal the writing in question; but how could she have exculpated herself, she alone being aware of the contents and value, of which even the witness her master had employed, knew nothing? Some time elapsed, and the conspirators seemed no nearer their object, when the lord was seized with a violent illness. It threatened his life, and between its severer periods the old man set himself to the arrangement of his affairs. One night Anna, who watched him with an unwearying eye, saw him take from his strong box the paper of manumission, fold it in a cover, and seal and direct it. He then placed it in his bosom. Her nature, never a thoroughly bad one, warmed towards him at seeing this; for she entertained no doubt but that, contemplating the possibility of his death, he was about to repay her attentions by presenting her with the freedom of her son. Nor was she disappointed. The following day he summoned Demetrius to the bed-side, and placing in his mother's hand the document in its sealed cover, he informed the young man of its nature, and told him that Anna had richly earned it by her fidelity and care. He merely desired that the document might not be used until after his death, which, he truly said, would not detain them long. Demetrius departed, taking with him the precious instrument, and went to his cabin. The joint occupant of that dwelling was a person to whom I have scarcely referred, because nobody else connected with the story seems to have paid much attention to him; this was, however, Anna's husband. The young man, in his exultation, informed his reputed father of the boon which had been bestowed upon him; but the other, who had certainly no great reason to be pleased with the general conduct of his lord, affected to under-value the benefit, and even to cast doubts upon its reality. His sneers and scoffs so worked upon the mind of Demetrius, that, forgetful of his lord's injunction, he tore open the papers. The contents were a document of manumission, drawn up and attested in the most regular style—there could be no mistake as to the signature. The only defect was in the body of the writing, where was—not a blank, which Demetrius could easily have supplied—but another name than his own—the name of Gregoire Kuzma—a mere stopgap, as one might write John Smith or John Doe. Furious with indignation, he rushed back to the house, and found his mother weeping over the dead body of her master.

What could the slave do now? The influence of Anna had been used in vain, and was over. She was stupefied at hearing the news, but on her son's again examining the envelope of the document all was made clear to her. With the mocking writing, their owner had enclosed the letter from the Greek priest.

The mother's resolve had not given way. They retired to her cottage, and for some time lived together until those who had the administration of the estate arrived to take charge of it. The mother and son thought that it was desirable that Demetrius, who, as an able-bodied serf, would speedily be in

demand, should avoid meeting his new master. One of those
travelling pedlars who form an important means of communication among the slave class in Russia, had, it was observed, spent
much time in the cottage of Anna. On the night before the
day upon which a general muster of serfs was expected, Demetrius and the pedlar disappeared together. The former had
been supplied with a large share of the money which Anna had
contrived to scrape together, and, with a solemn promise to his
mother, he departed.

There is a certain part of the province of Bessarabia, in which
the population seems to consist entirely of patriarchs. To visit
the vicinity you would not perhaps notice the fact—indeed
appearances are against it; but the books of the Russian police
(which, in Russia at least, would be held as conclusive evidence
against any witness, oral or written, which could be produced
upon the face of the earth) testify that a wonderful number of
the people live to unheard-of ages. Never were so many " oldest
inhabitants" got together as in this obscure and seldom-traversed
district. The Russian newspapers, even, were allowed to remark
upon the strange healthiness of the place. Some of the people
live to be 100, others to 110, and even 120 and 130. The police,
of course, understand the matter, but it is not their business to
explain it.

In this happy district there lived, previously to the breaking
out of the " revolution" in 1832, a man apparently middle-aged,
and named Gregoire Kuzma. Any one who had known the
young Demetrius ——, would have detected a strong like-
ness between the two persons, if indeed they were two; but it
happened that none in the village in which Gregoire lived had
enjoyed the advantage of the young serf's acquaintance. It was
only known that he had regular police papers, and that, although he certainly did not seem so old by twenty years or so
as they described him, that was no business of the police, to
whom indeed Gregoire behaved exceedingly well. He so ingra-
tiated himself with them, that one day, when a large packet from
Podolia arrived by post, and turned out to be a document manu-
mitting Gregoire Kuzma, duly signed and attested, the whole

batch of officials were quite radiant in their congratulations—did
not invent above half the usual number of unnecessary obstacles
in the way of the recognition of the document, nor fleece the
fortunate holder out of about twice the amount of fees permitted
by law. Such a case of forbearance was quite unknown even in
the memory of the oldest inhabitant there. The formalities
were completed, and Gregoire Kuzma was a free man. By a
curious coincidence, within a few days of the arrival of the manumission, a really old inhabitant, whose name was also Gregoire
Kuzma, and whose death had been daily expected for a long
time, departed this life. The younger Kuzma was with him a
good deal about the time the former first appeared in the place,
and certainly paid him money. But to say that the younger
man was Demetrius ——, and that he purchased the other
man's name and police papers, and thus prepared himself for the
reception of his paper of manumission—or to hint that such things
are often done, and that a document passed from an old man to a
young one unites the periods of two lives, and that when the
young one becomes old he must, according to the police books, be
very old indeed, and that the officials cannot see such things when
pieces of gold are placed before their eyes—would be a series of
hasty assertions, founded upon the assumption that the police
system of Russia has its weaknesses, which is clearly impossible.

One fine morning, some months later, the travelling pedlar
was again seen at Anna's cottage. Demetrius had redeemed his
promise, sending word to his mother that he was a free man.
And the Count ——, who had in some measure retrieved his
fortune by successes at cards, at which the adventures of his
earlier life made him so skilful that many persons were timid
enough to refuse to play with him, more than once met his former slave in very good society in St. Petersburg, and—must one
add it?—cheated him sadly at various games of chance and skill.
But he will not do so any more, because Demetrius, or rather
Gregoire, having been foolish enough to mix himself up with the
revolutionary movements of 1832 (in which he distinguished
himself by great animosity against all serf-owners who were
accustomed to flog their slaves), is at present located in Siberia.

CHAPTER V.

WE now come to a closer survey of Russian agriculture, as displayed in the vast and fertile provinces of Podolia and Kiev —to which, as its system is similar, we may add the province of Wolhynia. The three divisions I have named are conjointly the great corn-producing districts of the empire, and a description applicable to one is, with unimportant differences, applicable to the whole. These three provinces, at this moment shaven and bare, afford, towards harvest season, a wonderful display. Regions apparently illimitable stretch away on every side, presenting in unrivalled vastness the spectacle of a sea of waving corn—an expanse whose wealth the eye, overpowered with its hugeness, vainly struggles to embrace and to appreciate. There ripens the treasure of the thousand granaries of Europe—there rolls the golden flood destined to break upon a hundred shores.

The land upon which this mighty harvest waves is, generally speaking, the property of Polish gentlemen of "noble" birth. The estates into which it is divided are usually very large, and are inhabited by a population of serfs, whose residences are congregated in villages. In certain cases these estates are in the hands of intendants, or of farmers holding under the original owners, and in not a few instances the revolutionary movements of recent years have placed the property in the possession of the Crown, by means of the confiscations which followed the suppression of the insurrections. But these last-mentioned estates contribute, as a rule, but little towards the uniformity of the fertile scene, or to the wealth of the province in which they are situated, and this for reasons which will appear presently. The first described estates—namely, those in the possession of Polish noblemen, and cultivated by their serfs—form the far greater portion of the region the characteristics of which we are now to consider.

In laying the soil of these districts nature has been most kind. A fine rich mould, varying in depth, which, however, is always considerable, rests either upon an argillaceous basis, or upon one of calcareous stone. The various landowners of whom I have sought information, have habitually admitted that their soil is, naturally, unexceptionable for corn purposes. And, upon their opinion of its merits, they defend a practice which the English farmer will scarcely believe possible. Little manure is used in these countries, at least for the purpose of fertilization. It is thrown away—treated as a nuisance ; and the agriculturist does not scruple to avow his conviction—first, that the land does not and cannot require manuring; and secondly, that the soil would be actually injured by such application. With my English habits of reverence for the agent thus unworthily treated—having, in boyish days, seen it placed in literary juxtaposition with the most revered of all things, and having many a time transcribed the apothegm, that " money, like manure, was only valuable when spread"—I was scarcely prepared to believe that an article so honoured in England could be so scorned in Russia. My investigations have therefore been the more searching. The result has confirmed the statement originally made. Manure is not used, as such, in the corn provinces of Russia. It *is* used, however —if use the practice may be called—upon certain occasions; and it is employed in a fashion which I suppose will scarcely be considered more enlightened than that of entirely rejecting it.

" There are no real roads in these provinces." So I was told, on turning my attention, as naturally happens very early in an inquiry into the condition of a country, to the means of transit afforded for its produce; and the statement has been confirmed by representatives of all classes of inhabitants of the provinces in question. Road-making, in the merely agricultural districts of Russia, appears to be a science utterly unknown. The following is as nearly as possible a literal translation of the words of one of the best informed and most enlightened of the gentlemen to whom I addressed myself:—

" Roads—no, we have no roads. Not roads as the word is understood among yourselves, you English, or as in France, or any where but among ourselves. It would not answer. To make a good road is a most expensive process, as you must very well know, coming from England. We have a simpler course than to gather together materials and build a pathway ; for it is really building to make these ways as they are generally made. Observe, we do not need them. Not, of course, that it is not necessary that our waggons and carts and carriages should have a path, but we can supply that without much trouble. Land is not so valuable with us but that we can afford more for our transit than the strips of ribbons which you call roads in England, and which I have seen. We do not enclose our track. Its direction is clear enough, but its sides can hardly be called defined. Certainly," he said, laughing, " we have not hedges for jumping over by the hunters, or posts and rails to be stolen by the peasants. The course is wide and open. If the waggons and the carts tear it up, or the rains make it impassable in one place, it is easy to deflect a little to the right hand or the left, and to make a fresh track. That costs nothing. So that we have very good paths, after all."

In answer to my observation, that such good paths must become very bad paths in bad weather, he said—

" No doubt rain makes ground wet, and wet ground is not good for travelling. But observe, firstly, that at the times when we have bad weather we are not chiefly engaged in carrying. Storms may come, but they are accidents, and, as we say, in the hands of God. But it is not generally bad weather when our roads are mostly in use. Secondly, observe, we have means of mending very bad places in the roads, and of doing so at small expense."

" With stones, or gravel, or what?"

" Neither stones nor gravel ; we have another way. There is this manure, which you are so anxious we should learn to mix up with I know not what cookery of M. Liebig and others— and that it should help to make our corn grow. Well, we do not wish that—perhaps we do not comprehend the cookery of your M. Liebig. But we make the manure useful sometimes, for all that. We lay it down in the roads, where the weather has made the holes very bad, and it becomes very useful at once."

" And when it gets saturated with wet, the place is worse than before."

" By that time the chief work of the season is done, probably, and if not we can put down more. But I tell you the roads answer our purpose very well. If we had railroads I don't give an opinion as to what would happen. I do not think they would answer. But, assuredly, we are not likely to follow your system in England."

" But it seems to me that such paths as these must make travelling very slow. It must take weeks for a waggon of corn to make the journey from your own estate to Odessa."

" Corn is a quiet traveller, my dear friend, and complains not, Also, it travels fast enough, and as fast as other people's. You see you cannot make me discontented with our roads."

Another landowner to whom I applied, and who had travelled a good deal in various parts of Europe, fully confirmed the foregoing account, but by no means took so good-natured a view of it.

" The paths have this advantage," he said; " there is grass upon them for the bullocks that draw the waggons. As for corn, I say nothing. But as to the rest, I can only say that I my-self have frequently, when travelling in my carriage, stuck in the roads for hours and hours, and I remember it once required twelve bullocks to pull me and my family out of one of the sloughs. To be sure, bullock labour is cheap enough."

Demand of whom I would, and as to whatever portion of these vast provinces I could mention, the reply was the same—" We have tracks, but no roads." Some of the witnesses appeared to consider the fact a subject for regret, and others had scarcely considered it at all. In more than one case, the *immediate* reply was, that the roads were very good indeed; but this was a mere impression which speedily yielded, by the frank admission of the speakers themselves, when they came to remember and to describe

the actual condition of the soil, and the rate of travelling. But
the landowners in these corn-producing provinces do not see
that the want of real roads in their country is, under the ex-
isting state of things, any practical evil. Nor could they—this
is almost a needless addition to the preceding remark—be easily
brought to any outlay, either of labour or of capital, which should
simply have for its object an improvement of the means of transit.
They live upon the sale of their corn, and the roads, as they
exist, afford a slow, but tolerably sure means of travel for the
bullock-waggon of the serf during the seasons of transit; the
corn is, sooner or later, housed in the granaries of Odessa; and
it would be difficult to show these gentlemen how such an addition could be made to that result as would justify the investment of precious capital in the formation of a newfangled road.

Of the "roads" of the Steppe, which extend for upwards of a
hundred miles around us here, I have already spoken. I have
described them as about as discouraging as any practicable paths
well can be. But the evidence of numerous witnesses assures
me, that the Steppe roads are frequently far better than those
which run through the rich and fertile regions of which we are
speaking. Nor will this, upon consideration, be thought im-
probable; the nature of the two soils being remembered. The
very character of the land upon which the luxuriant harvests of
corn are supplied renders it unfit for purposes of traffic, while
the dried and parched Steppe region affords, at all events, a surer
pathway. To counterbalance this advantage, however, the frequent sterility of the latter makes it too often a terrible road for
the unfortunate animals who traverse it; and this is a point
which must not be omitted in the general estimate of the transit
means at the disposal of the Russian. Of course, in the limited
distances of our own country, where the space between town
and town is nothing formidable; the question whether grass
grows by the roadside is interesting only to the gipsy with his
donkey, or the travelling showman with his bare-boned pony.
But in speaking of districts of vast size, and infrequent population, the matter assumes another aspect. When the bullock-
waggons return from Odessa to the estates whence they have

come laden with corn, the place of the discharged load is supplied with hay. As I write, the rain is streaming in dense torrents upon a string of fifteen of these waggons, piled to the height of seven or eight feet with hay, and on their way homewards. The present rain, which has been of but two or three days' duration, will possibly not affect the Steppe roads; but should it continue, the effect of which I have heard sorrowful stories will occur. The road is rendered difficult by the wet, and the journey is mercilessly protracted. The hay which is bought for the support of the bullocks will be exhausted—who, if fully fed, of course quickly use up their provender, and if underfed are incapable of the exertion requisite to shorten the journey—the grass of the Steppe has long since vanished—and the poor animals will die of exhaustion and ultimate starvation, as happens to great numbers when the ordinary obstacles of the road are increased. This it may be well to remember, when considering the road question. It should be added that the landowner has no direct interest in this part of the question, the bullocks being the property of the serf himself, who has engaged to transport the corn.

We will now proceed to the question of actual cultivation. In speaking of the vast unbroken sea of corn which meets the eye of the spectator, in one of the provinces of which we are speaking, on every side, it should be observed that the description applies only to what is termed a bird's-eye view. But, could he survey the country from a point which would allow him to combine a general *coup d'œil* with close observation—he would remark that a very considerable portion of the land below him was out of cultivation.

The course of cultivation is this. The Russian farmer divides his land into three parts, equal or unequal according to circumstances, but, from necessity, of no very great difference. In the same year he sows one of these divisions with wheat, a second with oats or barley, and the third remains fallow. In the next year the division previously sown with wheat is sown with oats, the oats division is left fallow, and the fallow division is sown with wheat. In the third year, which completes the farming cycle, the wheat division of the first year is fallow, the oats division of the first year is sown with wheat, and the fallow division of the first year, being of course the wheat division of the second year, is sown with oats. Thus the rotation is formed, and thus it will appear that one-third of the farmer's land is constantly out of cultivation.

The vast size of the estates in these provinces enables the agriculturist thus to recruit his land in some degree by allowing it these incessant holidays. And this system affords the means by which the Russian farmer is enabled to dispense with manure. "What should I manure my land for?" said a many-acred nobleman to me; "when it has done its work for the present I can lay it aside, and take to it again when refreshed."

It is not for me to express an agricultural opinion upon the system. In the judgment of many well-informed landowners even here, this system is gradually found to impoverish the soil. It is difficult—in fact, it is impossible—in Russia, to arrive with exactitude at any result solely depending on figures; for there are no persons who esteem themselves sufficiently interested in a general view of a subject to take the pains without which such data cannot be procured; while, unluckily, there are many persons who, from various causes, are mischievously active in impeding, if not in entirely choking up, various channels of information. But the general impression is abroad, that the land of the corn district, originally so rich, is becoming impoverished under the system to which it is subjected; that the produce, although there may be no obvious difference in the returns of a port, nor any actual economizing in the outlay of a nobleman, is not what it used to be, and that, some time or other—the usual date at which it is proposed to commence alterations in Russia—a change of system will become necessary. Meantime, so long as the landowner can keep apparently up to the average mark, he is satisfied.

But the system of cultivation will be better understood when I have adverted to the relation the labourer bears to the soil. The Russian serf, as I have said, is, to all real intents and purposes, the absolute property of his master. Nominally and publicly, and in the private conversation of those who know themselves to be under official cognizance, it is the custom to speak of him as a being attached to the soil—one of the *adscripti glebæ*—and by no means as in the condition which Englishmen understand as slavery. It is not worth while to cavil upon words. The serf is born a serf, is unable without his owner's leave to depart from the estate on which he is born, and is bound to give a large portion of his time and labour to the cultivation of that estate without fee, hire, or reward. He may not, according to law, be flogged by his owner beyond the amount of five lashes at a time; but, as a most kind-hearted owner of many thousand slaves said to me a few days since, " What signifies that restriction? The law provides that I shall give my slave only five lashes at a time. But the law does not say how far that 'time' shall be from the next 'time.' Suppose I supply the law's defect, and say five minutes, I do not think the serf is much a gainer by the law." In the sketch of the life of a serf in the last chapter, I also mentioned that, if a serf displeases his master, the latter has only to signify to the governor of the district that he wishes the offender transported to Siberia, and the government immediately charges itself with the care of the serf, conditionally only on the master becoming responsible for the expense of the transit to the place of transportation. But as this latter exercise of authority would simply deprive the owner of the estate of a piece of valuable property, it is not likely to be often exerted; it must, however, be mentioned in describing the condition of the serf, and in illustrating the position of these *adscripti glebæ.* To this must be added, although there is a show of denial of the fact, that a serf *can* be removed from estate to estate at the good pleasure of his proprietor, although an attempt at legislation, of which I shall presently speak, affected to place some restrictions upon this kind of removal.

The serf, therefore, is the unpaid labourer, by whose assistance the lord cultivates his land, and produces the corn which is poured into Odessa. Now, great numbers—indeed the majority —of the noblemen to whom these provinces belong, retain the management of the estates in their own hands, and direct the agriculture, aided of course by the usual officials. The large size of the estates is in no small degree maintained by the policy of the Government of Russia, which is determinately opposed to the subdivision of landed property, as being likely to aid in producing a fusion between classes whom it is considered far better to keep apart, estranged, and even hostile. Not long since a gentleman left ten sons, among whom his property would have been apportioned in the usual way—when it was signified by authority that it either was or would be held contrary to the interpretation of Russian law, that any estate should be subdivided below a certain point, and that such an arrangement must be made as would preserve the property in respectable integers. It is, therefore, upon a grand scale that the system of serf-cultivation, be it good or bad, is usually conducted. Although it is not easy to lay down any standard of size, it may be convenient to mention that, whereas the possession of "one hundred souls" (the regular and authorised term) is the smallest which entitles an individual to be considered a landowner, the possession of two thousand "souls" implies the holding of a very large estate.

These people reside in cottages, generally similar in form, but differing in comfort according to the means and habits of the occupant. To each serf enough land must be allotted for his own support, and that of his family. The lord has the sole right of setting apart this allotment; and he formerly possessed, and often exercised, the right of varying it at whatever time and season he pleased; but this power has been in some sort restricted, as we shall see.

The ordinary quantity of labour exacted from the Russian serf, was formerly precisely that which it pleased his lord to demand. But this condition of things has been amended—for every thing between superior and inferior is amended, that is reduced to any species of rule ; and custom, and the attempt at legislative interference already alluded to, have practically settled the time at about three days in the week. It amounts to somewhat less in certain portions of the provinces, where, I am informed, it sometimes does not exceed two days. On three days the serf works for his lord—on the remaining days of the week he is at liberty to cultivate his own ground for his own support.

The farming implements with which the serf performs his agricultural duties, not only upon the land allotted to himself, but—and this is worthy of remark—upon the estate of his lord, are the serf's own property. They are his own in a peculiar way. For when he fails in performance of his duty, or in making any payment which he may have contracted for—and the lord has the power of evicting him from his cottage, and of sweeping away all that he has in the world—an exception must be made in favour of his farming implements—a term to which rather a large significance is given in an agricultural population. The "tools of a man's trade" are protected, under certain circumstances, in England; but it is curious to see that, in the middle of a slavery like that of Russia, a similar exemption should be afforded. It is, I am informed, rigidly preserved, and the implements are "sacred against the master." But it should be noted that, the culture of the land being carried on with instruments belonging to the ignorant and pauperised serf, there is small chance of any of the improvements of modern science finding their way into the soil of Russia. The serf himself would consider it—as the wretched Irish peasant considers it— a species of irreligion to fall away from his father's creed in the matter of a plough or a dung-fork. But I do not know that, in many instances, had the landowner to find the implements, there would be much difference. There is the same adherence to old rules in landlord as in serf, though from different reasons. The serf remains what his father and grandfather were, and does as they did, from sheer ignorance; but the landowner refuses to move, from a resolute determination that no outlay of capital which can, by any earthly resistance, be avoided, shall be risked upon his estate. I am acquainted with the case of an exceedingly wealthy landowner—one whose fortune cannot be less than £15,000 a year—who was recently counselled to introduce upon his estate an agricultural instrument considered a necessary on almost every farm in England, and his answer was—

G

"*Mon Dieu!* look at the expense. Why, you are asking me to lay out nearly sixty pounds! No, no; we'll keep to the old plan."

There are, however, two sides to the question of the land-owner's unwillingness to invest capital in his land, and I shall, before concluding this part of the subject, bring forward the statement advanced by those who are not to be accused of avarice, and hardly of shortsightedness. But we will, in the first place, proceed with the matter immediately under consideration. As regards the draining of these vast districts, I need hardly say that, hearing what I had heard, I did not expect that the witnesses I examined would have any very satisfactory account to give. But nature, who so often helps those who will not help themselves (to the great discontent of those who will, and the unsettling their convictions as to the duty of industry), has in some degree anticipated the negligence of the Russian farmer. The great corn-producing districts are not only so diversified with gentle slopes and undulations as to be in some sort provided with assistance to drainage; but, as if it had been foreseen that it is of no use merely to assist the Russian—you must do his work for him—the country itself abounds with a series of natural dykes, which in wet seasons accumulate great quantities of the superfluous moisture. And although, of course, some application of science to the object of drainage would improve the kindly provisions of nature into an admirable system, the present state of matters is, as regards the land itself, by no means so unsatisfactory as might be expected from the neglect by the population of the ordinary means. Of course, these dykes, or natural water-courses, are abandoned to the chances which govern other things here—where they intersect a "road," the passage is usually difficult, and sometimes dangerous—the bridges which are thrown over them are of the most miserable description—and a traveller who has known them often inquires, with no small trepidation, while the horses are being put to his carriage, whether he will be obliged to cross a dyke that stage. A Russian lady—to whose kindness I would gladly bear a more distinct testimony, but that it would be no friendly return to indicate, in Russia, an individual who had given a stranger information of the smallest of its shortcomings—told me that one day, travelling in the heart of one of the provinces we are speaking of, the carriage came to a dead stop. Her own servant was probably asleep, for one of the postilions presented himself, and announced that a dyke was before them, which there were two ways of crossing, and he requested Madame's orders.

" But why do you ask me?" replied the lady; "take, of course, the safest way."

Still the postilion was unsatisfied. He was willing to take either course, but he could wish the responsibility removed from his shoulders. The case stood thus:—The dyke was crossed by a wooden bridge; but this was at once so rickety and so rotten, that there was considerable probability that it would give way with the weight of the carriage, in which case—

" *Mon Dieu!*—yes; and the other way ?"

The other way was *through* the dyke, which had, however, been swoln by rain, and the carriage might either swim, if the wheels did not touch the bottom, or might be half filled with water if they did. Under these circumstances——

The lady was in despair, and was perhaps thinking of trying her fate by the *sortes* (only that the censorship proscribed all books written by any body, except writers never suspected of being conjurers), when, on the opposite bank of the dyke, she saw some travellers with carts, who seemed also in doubt how to proceed. They appeared inclined to give her the *pas*—but the maxim *fiat experimentum in corpore vili*, or its spirit, came strongly upon her mind, and the lady determined that the plebeians should cross first. So they sounded the water with poles, and shook their heads, and then traversed the frail bridge, and shook their heads again. Finally, they took engineering measures of considerable ingenuity, for, having some boards in their carts, they laid them over the worst holes in the bridge, and then fetched a quantity of manure from a neighbouring heap, and laid it over all, so as to make a tolerably smooth-looking, easy road. Then with fear and trembling, as true believers cross Al Sirat, they crossed, and Madame (not forgetting to pay toll to the rustic Telfords and Tierney Clarks) crossed also. But nobody should ever be in a hurry in Russia, except the Emperor.

Of the general character of the Russian system of farming, I could not prevail upon any of the defenders of the system to speak with any thing like dispraise; although, when pressed with questions founded upon my acquaintance with what we term good farming in England and in Scotland, it was obvious that they conceived much time and labour were thrown away by our own agriculturists, and, in consequence, that the improvements of our own country are unknown or unheeded in Russia; and of what we call clean farming they had obviously no idea, and conceived it a species of coxcombry. At the period of the year at which I write, a personal inspection of the provinces of which I speak would be useless—if, indeed, their distance and vastness, and the difficulty of travelling from point to point, did not render such an examination impracticable within any reasonable limits of time. But I believe myself to have obtained a closer insight into the system of Russian agriculture, than I could have gained by months of wandering over the soil itself. I have availed myself of somewhat unusual facilities for obtaining access to individuals connected with the land, as owners, as agents, and as labourers. I have derived my information from the very sources whence alone I could have hoped to gain it had I explored the districts themselves, while I have also had additional important assistance. I have sought the aid of the owners of large estates and numerous serfs, and I have talked (through an interpreter) with numbers of the serfs themselves as they arrived from their distant districts, and on their return; while I have also fortunately been made acquainted with several persons who, for purposes of business and with other objects, have resided in the provinces we speak of. And, were it not for the system which renders it worse than dangerous for a Russian subject to be known as giving the species of information which I have desired—a system which has compelled many gentlemen with whom I have been in intercourse to see me with precautions to which I need not refer, and has caused it to be matter of general request that " no names may be mentioned"—I could supply a long list of authorities for all that I have said, or may say. I do not suppose that, though this explanation may be surplusage to any one who knows Russia, it is altogether unnecessary as accounting to the general reader for the absence of names, and other specific indications.

I have said that the lord is not always the landlord of the estates. The change in proprietorship—I use the word advisedly —is made for the time being by means of a lease, which is frequently granted to some other person, who may be disposed to manage the estate, or a part of it. There is a rule restraining the indiscriminate grant of such leases. The person to whom a lease is granted takes the place of the lord, and must be in all respects clothed with his powers as regards the serfs on the estate. It is therefore necessary that he should be in the same rank as the lord—that is, he must not be a serf, for he has to rule serfs, and he must not be a Jew or heathen, for he has to rule Christian men. The same rule, I am informed, applies to the appointment of an intendant, when the lord desires to absent himself; and as such appointment must in all cases be submitted to and approved by the authorities, who insist upon knowing in whose care a mass of serfs are left, and upon taking order that such person shall be one on whom Government can depend, there is little chance of evading this rule. But notwithstanding the vigilance of authority, the rule excluding Jews, at least, is continually broken, as the possession of wealth enables the holders to overleap most earthly barriers here as elsewhere. The Jew is tolerated in Russia, and that is all—but he contrives, by the substitution of other names and other agencies, to manage many a hundred head of Christian serfs. The farmer, however, to whom the lease is granted, and whose name appears in the public registry, must fulfil the conditions required by law.

And here let me mention, that the Russians have anticipated us in reference to a registry of deeds and documents. The farmer's lease of which I speak, is not only upon stamped paper, and duly signed by the necessary parties, but to give it validity it is registered in the local court of the district where the property assigned is situated. And the same remark applies, *mutatis mutandis*, to all contracts, mortgages, sales, and other formalities and it is stated to me, that a Russian title to property may be completely investigated from books to which the public has access.

The lease of an estate is for three, six, or nine years ; but three is the most usual term. At its expiration the farmer will have tried the system of cultivation explained in the earlier part of this letter, " all round," and will be able to decide whether he shall ask for a renewal of a grant of land with which he has then had the fullest opportunity of becoming acquainted. The serf usually finds the new *locum tenens* any thing but a satisfactory exchange from the original lord, who is better known upon the estate, and more interested, of course, in the welfare of the peasantry. The farming proprietor has but one object, that of making as much out of the estate during his holding as possible ; and whatever relaxation of rights may ever be made, as regards the demand of labour and other service, it is not often made by the substituted lord.

There is another lord, who must by no means be omitted from the list—viz., the Crown. I am not now speaking of that headship as applicable to the case of what are termed Crown serfs, as their condition will be separately noticed ; but I allude to the Crown in the capacity of proprietor of confiscated estates. It is not necessary here to advert to the circumstances which produced the outbreaks in which so many Polish nobles took so prominent a part. It is enough to say, that among these gentlemen were some of the wealthiest and most respected landowners of Russia. The revolt crushed, the property of those engaged in it was seized, whether in town or country. Here, in Odessa, one of the finest buildings of the town—and one which early catches the eye, and leads one to believe the place a museum or public library—was built as a granary and store by one of these nobles ; but the government has appropriated it to military purposes. The magnificent house of the same noble is also converted into a government office. In the country the confiscations were upon a large scale. Of these appropriations it is difficult to say who can complain—the insurgents, as Colonel Talbot says to Waverley, of the Highlanders of 1745, had their eyes open to the game. " They threw for life or death, coronets or coffins, and could not claim to draw stakes because the dice had gone against them." But the population upon the forfeited estates found the change for the worse. The government, anxious not to throw the land out of cultivation, sought to manage the estates by means of commissioners of its own, who were put into the places of the extirpated nobility. The result might easily have been predicted, and was not slow in coming. The *employé* system, fastening upon the unlucky serfs, worked the most wretched oppression and job-bing—the exactions were terrible, and yet the Crown reaped little advantage. The peasant, brought into contact and collision with a class of men who had no interest in him or the estate, but whose only aim was self-enrichment, had no chance of fair play ; and he might, probably, have suffered somewhat longer, only that he was found to be suffering in vain. But as it was obvious that the Crown revenues were being plundered, and that the estates were likely to be something worse than merely unprofitable, it was resolved to change the system. The *employés* gave way to the soldiery. The government established upon their estates a kind of military colony. This can scarcely be called a retro-grade step; for though the estates are no longer, I believe, cul-tivated for profit, but simply for the support of that portion of the army placed upon it, the administration is said to be better and more humane than under the griping reign of the commis-sioners. But the withdrawing so many of the inhabitants of these estates from the general agricultural occupations of the country, has decidedly had one deleterious effect upon the corn trade. It has aided to raise the expense of transit (as I showed in an earlier chapter), and, combined with the effects of recent terrible mortality among the cattle used for drawing, supplies another item for discussion when the indirect hindrances to in-creased supply are under consideration.

There is also another mode of management of estates, which I will not omit, although instances of it are at present rare. It sometimes occurs that a lord, either from want of success in farming, or from want of taste in the pursuit, or because his presence may be needed elsewhere, calls his serfs together, and proposes to them to manage the estate among themselves. He, of course, being well aware of its capabilities, makes the best bargain he can, and the community, binding themselves to pay him the remuneration decided on, take the estate into their own hands. They take it only in an administrative capacity, and not with any delegation of the lord's own powers, which cannot devolve upon a serf. And in this manner the estate is managed —the remittances going to St. Petersburg, or Paris, or wherever the owner is located, and the serfs doing the best they can for themselves with the remaining profits. This plan is, I am told, not often adopted, although I believe that it has been found to work pretty well. One reason why it is not extensively pursued is to be found in the policy of the State, which has no great opinion of the absentee system, and is exceedingly chary of granting to any of its children permission to travel, far less to remain abroad. And as no person can quit Russia without proper papers, the check is easy. I am aware of cases in which very distinguished persons, by no means out of favour at head-quarters, have for years been soliciting permission to visit England and France, but the necessary sanction has invariably been refused—of course with the utmost politeness, and not unfrequently upon grounds with which it was impossible to quarrel, but the restraint, courteous or stern, is still the same. And a landowner will scarcely care to abandon his estate simply for the sake of living in another part of the empire.

The residence of the landowner in these provinces does not much resemble the château of France, or the country seat of England. But it is a dwelling in which comfort is found, and the word is well understood in Russia, where, I am bound to say (in the presence of many absurdities), certain contrivances, lacking among ourselves, for making home agreeable, may be discovered in every residence you enter. The Russian's stove warms his house all over, and the Russian's double windows keep out the winds and the draughts. In the districts to which I refer, the house, as a general rule, is extensive, but seldom consisting of more than one story. To the original plan each owner adds what he imagines himself to require, and the architectural irregularity of the edifice is of small consequence where there are no critical eyes. The house is surrounded by a large garden, but this is not a collection of grass-plots smooth as billiard-tables, or walks hard and sparkling with brilliant gravel, but is chiefly used as a kitchen-garden. The service of the house is performed by the domestic serfs, who are usually numerous, and whose functions are very much subdivided—a system which, so far as I have seen it in operation, does not carry with it the usual advantages of the division of labour, but has more affinity with the old Spanish practice of the multiplication of offices, which once—story says—caused a Sovereign to be toasted because there was nobody near whose duty allowed him to interfere. But the system of domestic economy of course varies with the master, and still more with the mistress; for whilst, in some houses which I have visited, I found that the obedience of the servants, though always given, was given in the way least pleasant, and that in others every servant seemed to be doing the work of some other official than himself, I have also seen' the serfs discharging the work of the house with as much cheerful- ness, noiselessness, and precision as we are in the habit of expect- ing in England. These household serfs, being constantly in contact with their owners, acquire better manners than the class out of doors—frequently "take pains with themselves," as the phrase is—and, after long and good service, are often rewarded with the present of their freedom. They are not, as a body, remarkable for honesty; but some of them I have heard very highly commended in this respect, and their natures, under kindly treatment, develop into a cheerfulness and cordiality which it is pleasant to see. Among themselves they are full of liveliness and merriment, and the least trifle is sufficient to occasion a startling shout of mirth in the serf's apartments—a noise which at first surprises the stranger, accustomed to the order and quiet of home, but of which the owners of the house either take no notice, or evince an interest in its cause. The manners of the domestics are apparently far less restrained in the presence of their superiors than with us—I do not mean

that there is any want of respect, but the tone is far more con-
versational than is encouraged in England, where Mrs. Gabriel
Varden's axiom is usually a sort of golden rule for servants
—" Answering me, Miggs, and providing yourself, is one and
the same thing." If a serf conceives himself, or especially herself,
better informed than the person giving instructions, I have
never seen that serf display the slightest hesitation in arguing
the case in question. The obvious devotion of the household
serf, male and female, to the children of the family is a pleasant
sign. In one family which I had the pleasure of visiting, I
noticed that one of the nursery-maids in attendance on a child of
the house was disfigured with scars, to an extent which made
her almost hideous. I am somewhat of a convert to the
doctrines of Mademoiselle de Cardoville, at least as regards the
appearance of those who are placed around children—and probably may have looked twice at the very ill-favoured maiden in
question, for the mistress of the house said, laughing—

" I am afraid that M. B—— is not admiring our poor Teckla?"

" Speaking frankly, one's admiration is probably due to your
attendant's intrinsic merits."

" It is, indeed," said the lady earnestly, " and I am glad to
have an opportunity of telling you so. She was, four years ago,
as pretty a girl as you are likely to see among our peasants. Our
house in the country took fire one night, and a considerable portion was destroyed; but every body was saved, and indeed the
person who had most to regret the accident, was Teckla there.
We were all standing looking at the conflagration, when it
rushed into Teckla's brain that this child here, then a baby, was
left behind in the burning house. She set up a wild shriek,
which frightened us more than the fire had done, and sprang into
the building through a window, the wood-work of which was in
flames. Forcing her way through the smoke, she managed to
penetrate into one of the bed-rooms, and there she must have
fallen down overpowered. She was got out with great difficulty,
and not until another side of the room to which she pushed had
given way, and she was discovered lying near a bed, with the
child's bed-cover in her hand. She must have madly snatched

at that, and then dropped. She was dreadfully burned, and her life was despaired of, but she ultimately recovered, though disfigured as you see. Her own account is, that she looked round for us all, missed the baby (she had been carried into a neighbouring cottage), and remembers nothing else."

I did not ask whether Teckla was still a serf, but the character of the lady with whom she was, and that of her husband, were guarantees that the faithful girl was, or would be, precisely in the position best for her, and deserved by her.

The last point to which I shall advert in this letter, is the demarcation of the boundaries of the estates. These divisions would more than puzzle the acutest land surveyor who ever fixed a rental upon rods, poles, and perches. "We have no hedges for jumping over by hunters," said an informant, whom I have already quoted, who, by-the-by, seemed to think that we were at last making some little progress in agriculture in England, when I told him that many English farmers were beginning to consider the hedge as a thing to be "put down." Nor have the Russians stone walls, like those which Irish horses go over like cats, touching the top. It would be difficult for a stranger to say that the estates were divided at all. But a description, obligingly furnished to me by an eyewitness of what he tells, will best explain how this department is managed :—

"I was invited to spend some days with the three sons of a deceased friend, whose large estate was to be divided between the young gentlemen, and the ceremony of partition was what I was asked to see. The affair was made the excuse for great hospitality, not only to the aristocracy but to the population around. For several days we had all sorts of festivities, and open house was kept for all who chose to come. The serfs got very tipsy and very uproarious; and if their betters did any thing in the same way, I beg you will attribute it to the humane motive of not wishing to discourage their inferiors by a display of too much perfection. One morning I was awoke by a great shouting and drumming, and looking out, I found a motley kind of procession, with flags and music, about the house. I dressed, and soon discovered that the great event, the dividing the estate, was really to come off. We started, most of the gentlemen on horseback, and I think there was a carriage or two, but the "following" was on foot. We had various officials with us, besides land-bailiffs, surveyors, and I don't know what other attendant gentry. Presently we came to a sort of long mound, which I should hardly have noticed, but which it appeared marked one side of the estate, and the authorities conferred together, and by certain signs and references to the points of the compass, agreed upon its identity. I had scarcely remarked that a great number of the peasantry had long slender wands in their hands—but at this moment all these wands were shaken as by common excitement, and the bearers rushed towards the mound, all apparently trying to hit a blow at something. I heard a desperate screeching, drowned in shouts of laughter, and pushing my horse into the crowd, I saw, trying to escape from the mound on which he had been tossed, a boy, of twelve or fourteen, who was certainly receiving as sound a flagellation, though administered amid roars of merriment, as a young gentleman of that age would desire. Every body was cutting at him, and he was so hemmed in that he had no chance of escape, the less that he was encumbered by his drapery, which had been disarranged, in scholastic fashion, that the castigation might more effectually reach the quarter for which it was chiefly destined. Well, the lad, having received a goodly memento of the place, was allowed to go away, which he did, running and roaring, both in good style. Requesting a little enlightenment, one of the most animated of the operators said—

" ' He will say to his grandson—that is the south boundary of the land—I know it well, and I shall never forget it, for I was well whipped upon it, thank God, fifty years ago.'

" And this pleasing ceremony of beating the bounds (of course varying the victim) we performed at a vast number of places during the morning's ride. We found mounds around the estate, and at each of these, some lad green enough to be caught, underwent Spartan discipline, but by no means in Spartan silence. And where the new boundaries were to be made, which had obviously been arranged beforehand, fresh mounds were thrown

up, and other lads had the honour of being the first to be fusti-
gated thereon. Never was such a flogging-day since the seventy
young gentlemen of Westminster school were all whipped the
same morning. Then we all returned to the mansion, and the
jovialties of preceding nights were outdone by all who had
taken part in the affecting ceremonial, with the exception, I
suppose, of the young gentlemen, who had not even the comfort
left to sit them down and cry."

CHAPTER VI.

WE will now examine the condition of the agricultural labourer in Russia, that labourer being a serf.

The nation of serfs, although now in circumstances, social and physical, which afford little apparent promise of elevation of character, individual or national, is not entirely without its traditions and recollections. Its songs, still preserved, and characterised by a natural melody not unfrequently found linked to the legends of uncultivated races, speak of union, and happiness, and patriotism; all, however, antedated to the subjection of the original population of Russia. I have not been able to meet with any printed collection of these compositions, nor have those whom I have consulted any recollection that such exists; but I have had the words of several of the songs repeated to me, and it would not be difficult to throw them into a form which, coupled with the original airs, might make them acceptable even among the mass of so-called national melodies with which the invention of our composers at home teems so satisfactorily. In love-songs (I may also mention the fact as helping to illustrate the character of the people) the serf's minstrelsy is peculiarly rich; but, so far as my limited acquaintance with his lyrics goes, he does not seem to have found any thing new to say or sing upon a subject which, one way and another, has been a good deal discussed in its time. Beyond the delivery of sentiments of the order habitual to the inspirations "to be had in the theatre, price one shilling," the serf in love has not much in him; but, as might be expected, he occasionally goes further than the decorum of English audiences might think it discreet to follow him. He is also very religious, according to his lights, abstaining from work and adhering to whisky upon saints' days with extreme scrupulousness. The .species of devotion which he is likely to be taught by his priests (I speak of the lower class of course), is not likely to have much influence upon his daily walk and conversation; and its connection with the duties and restraints of life may be estimated by the fact, that the thief or burglar, when captured, and his proceedings traced, is often found to have visited the church in the way to the scene of his offence, and to have bespoken from one or other of the saints a benediction upon the tools of his vocation. There are few places devoted to the use of the serf in which you will not see some kind of religious image; the more expensive ones are manufactured in Italy, and consist of a sort of picture-frame, varying in size from six inches to two and three feet square, and a few inches deep—the front being of glass. Within is a blaze of gilding, leaves, flowers, garlands, and other devices, in the middle of which is usually the Virgin, sometimes holding the child, sometimes recumbent, and a host of little wax figures hanging about and over her, and intended to be regarded in the light of cherubim. Some of these shrines are very showy, others of a mean character, but the leading idea is always the same. The serf entering a place where one of them is hung up, never omits his reverence to it. The question of the attempt at fusing what was formerly the United Greek and Catholic Church with the Orthodox rankles in the serf's pious mind; and, I am told, is considered by him as one of his grievances, but it is a topic upon which it is not easy to get him to speak, except under another kind of spiritual influence, which deprives his theological speculations of much of their value.

I have said that the serf was entitled to an allotment of land sufficient for his support, and that of his family. This allotment, of course, varies in proportion to his requirements; but it is upon rather a large scale, taking the average, and a scale which will in some degree show the extent of the estates. The quantity, on the average, is usually what is called a *deciatine*, or nearly three acres. This the serf cultivates in his own way, and at such times as he is not doing his duty to his owner. Under a former *régime* the permanent possession of this ground by the

serf was very uncertain, the owner having, and frequently exer-
cising, the power of displacing and removing him at will, and at
times when such removal must entail upon the unlucky creature
the most disastrous consequences. But this, at least, has of late
been rendered difficult to the most arbitrary master.

For many years it has been the desire of the government to
take some step which should ameliorate the condition of the serf,
by rendering him somewhat more independent of the lord.
Even the emancipation scheme, as I have mentioned, found
favour for a time at headquarters, although subsequently laid
aside. But a measure which promised to bear some good fruit
was actually introduced some years since, and but for causes of
a peculiar character, would at this moment be in general operation. This was a government measure usually known as the
"Inventory." Its character, which would scarcely be gathered
from its ordinary title (any more than would the nature of our
own Statute of Frauds), was to adjudge and define the relative
position of lord and serf in regard to matters of property and
other details of serf-life. The general principle of the measure
was considered to be just, and the measure itself was approved
by many of the proprietors of estates. That the serf might be
enabled to avail himself of its provisions, it was ordered that in
each district to which it related three copies of the "Inventory"
should be kept for public inspection—one in the church, one at
the house of the priest, and one at the court-house—an arrangement which would apparently secure to the serf a knowledge of
his rights under the measure. But various agencies were at
work to defeat its operation. Not the least important, perhaps,
although a very common-place one, was its own voluminousness.
Keen-witted as the serf may be in matters concerning his own
interests, a mass of paper, fortified with law phrases, is a formidable barrier between him and an adversary. And though no
doubt the placing one copy of the measure in the hands of the
priest—who, being of the same faith with the parishioners,
whose guide, adviser, and friend he ought to prove himself,
might be expected to assist them in working out its objects in
opposition to any resistance by heretic lords—was designed to

confer advantage on the peasants, such has hardly been the
result. For the priest—needy, sordid, and cunning—has usually,
it appears, been found to play the game of the wealthy Catholic
lord rather than that of the poor Greek serf. And, once gained
over to the owner's side, it is not difficult to imagine into what
an abyss of error and perplexity a cunning priest, interpreting a
legal instrument, might plunge a whole village of helpless demi-
savages. The law has been greatly evaded or neglected, and at
present there seems no means of enforcing it more rigidly, were
the disposition of government inclined to further interference.
It has had a beneficial effect, however, in reference to two points
of importance—it has caused the creation of a very reasonable
species of tenant-right—that is, it prevents a serf from being
suddenly turned out of his holding, during any part of the year,
at the whim of his master; and it has tended to regulate the
periods at which the latter shall demand the serf's labour—the
old system affording no check whatever, and enabling the lord
to select precisely such days as might suit himself, or as the
state of the weather rendered advantageous, without regard to
the necessities of the serf, or the little harvest upon which he
depended for existence. On these two points, both of great
importance, the "Inventory" is stated to have exercised a
salutary authority.

It is not denied that the policy of the supreme authority in
Russia, is far from unfavourable to the welfare of the serf, or
that, if measures for his benefit could be carried into effect with
safety (a word of extended signification under the circumstances),
his condition would be materially ameliorated, and the land-
marks of right and remedy would be established around him.
It is not necessary to search for any secret motive for this
benevolent disposition in favour of the serf, or to contend, as is
unhesitatingly done by the landlords themselves, that it is, and
always has been, the policy of the crown to promote, as much as
possible, disunion and distrust between the lord and the serf.
It is not needful for me to dwell upon the fact that the Crown
discourages any attempt on the part of the lords themselves to
ameliorate the condition of the peasant; and indeed when it

H

was, at no distant period, discovered that the circulation of writings upon the subject had spread and confirmed an opinion, on the part of some of the landowners, that the initiative might advantageously be taken by themselves, very great disquiet was occasioned at St. Petersburg. A movement which should promote good feeling, and should create better ties than those of authority and servitude, between these two interests, was by no means acceptable to the third and dominant interest. But with this I have not, as it seems to me, much to do. From all that I can learn, there can be no doubt that the Emperor himself, however he may feel it necessary to adhere to a certain political system, is sincerely desirous to promote the happiness of his subjects, free and serf; and, without attributing any second motive, it may reasonably be believed that he would gladly avail himself of any opportunity of benefiting the millions, who look up to him with so strange a devotion. The discussion of the agencies which would clash with any such manifestation of the imperial will, is scarcely calculated for these letters.

But—and the chief purpose of the preceding paragraph is to lead to this statement—the landowner avails himself of the circumstance I have indicated, to justify *his* policy in dealing with the estates in his hands. Not one ruble of capital will he unnecessarily (as he interprets the term) lay out upon his land— not an improvement will he make—not an eye will he cast to the future welfare of the property; but he will continue the old system, year by year extorting from the land all that it will yield, but doing nothing further. In vain it is proved to him that a better system and better means of transit would in a course of years enormously increase the value of his estate, and enable him to transmit a noble inheritance to his children. He is not unwilling to admit the fact, but he justifies his refusal to risk a ruble upon a plea with which it is difficult for a stranger to deal. He has no confidence in the endurance of the social system upon which his present prosperity is founded; he has no certainty, he declares, that state policy, or servile revolution, may not deprive him of his serf-property. He holds on, and believes he does wisely in securing the harvest and housing it while he may—but he has seen too much, and has learned too much, to build upon the perpetuity of any thing around him. Such is the argument which is addressed in reply to the advice to "farm high." I have no reason to doubt that, in numerous cases, the conviction of insecurity does opperate to prevent improvement and outlay; but I also believe that, speaking generally, the spirit and habits of the landowner are opposed to any operation of which he does not see the instant result. He prefers "housing" his money. And I have, upon no scanty inquiry, and upon no hasty reflection, formed the conclusion, that from the present race of landowners in the great corn districts of Russia, we must look for no movement in the direction of· progress. We see what those districts can produce, as under the present system we see what they do produce—but in my judgment there is no present probability of their being enabled to do more.

The labourer's position, therefore—and, as will be observed, it is to bear upon this that I have thus briefly touched upon a subject which, discussed for its own sake, would demand far ampler handling—is likely to be stationary, except under the operation of influences on which it is impossible to calculate. So far as the landlord is concerned, the peasant must remain *in statu quo.* Let us, therefore, complete our examination of that *status.*

The serf, dependent for his subsistence upon his agricultural exertions, is usually found to be a creature of few wants beyond those within reach of his hands. He eats but little meat—a fact I have already adverted to in the case of the town-dwelling serf, and one which is worthy of remark in a country where the price of meat is so low. Vegetables of various kinds are his chief diet. In most cottages we find the *pot au feu*—that enduring and most excellent kitchen, which, if English landlords would teach their peasantry to adopt it, would confer a real blessing upon the latter; for nothing can be more savoury or more economical than the cookery of the *pot au feu*—nothing more wasteful or more monotonous than the cookery practised among the humbler class (when they obtain meat) in England.

The perpetual *pot au feu*, always ready, and yet always prepared, in the most catholic spirit, to receive any addition which good fortune .may bring, animal or vegetable—always redolent of an aroma, suggestive at once of nourishment and of flavour, and always preserving to the eater the best and most nutritious portions of the food confided to it—is a wholesome contrast to the English contrivances for getting as little as possible out of the best possible material. Of wheat, in a world of wheat, the serf knows nothing except as a costly article of commerce, his own rye-bread being ordinarily as dark and heavy as can well be imagined; though of this bread there are various qualities, and I have seen some which might take its place as one of the exceptions ordered " for a change" for the breakfast table at home. But the favourite food of the serf is a species of gruel, " thick and slab," made of the grits of buckwheat, and by no means bad to the taste—especially when flavoured, as it sometimes is, with vegetable condiments, of which one retains the smack for a couple of days. Millet is also much used by the peasant. Salted cucumbers—not the huge green *baton* with which the London supper-eater defies the nightmare—but small, hard things, of a few inches in length, and very bitter, are among his staple articles of food, as also is beet-root, which he devours to an amazing extent. Lard is also a very important feature in his housekeeping—it is plentifully used in his cookery, and for other purposes for which one would prefer engaging the assistance of butter. The drink of the serf is water, except when he can get *votki*, wherewith he loves, not to become gradually excited, but to stupefy himself has rapidly as he can—a slave Mokanna leaping at one spring into the " burning waters" of oblivion.

The house of the serf is usually built, in Podolia, of laths and mud, and thatched vilely; but elsewhere, and according to the resources of the district, it is either of stone, or of wood. The latter substance is used when the estate is in the neighbourhood of some of the vast forests which supply the serf with building materials, and his lord with delicious truffles. The floor of the house is of clay, and there is a chimney to carry away the smoke.

—

of the stove, which warms the single room in which the family huddle together through the dreadful nights of winter. Beyond the presence of exceeding dirt, there is nothing else of a character worth noting. I have, however, seen filthier hovels in Ireland than any I have yet seen in Russia, and I have noticed in the former country more evidences of an indisposition on the part of the peasant to help himself to the most ordinary comforts. Though, as I have said in an earlier letter, " a stitch in time" is by no means the habitual remedy of the Russians, still, if a hole comes in the wretched thatch of the Russian cottier, he sometimes scrambles up and re-thatches the spot—while the Irishman gets away from under the hole, so that the wet may not actually fall upon him, or, if he be of an unusually active character, he thrusts up into the hole some article of household use, not obviously wanted at the instant. The peasants of the two countries have, however, more point of resemblance than it is perhaps worth while to enumerate here.

As regards the moral condition of the serf, I fear that my report must be of a very unsatisfactory character. The causes of this will have already unfolded themselves. Utterly without secular instruction, and delivered over, for religious culture, to as depraved and worthless a priesthood as ever taught superstition to ignorance, what possible hope is there for the Russian agricultural serf? He is an habitual drunkard, and would be an habitual thief had he the opportunity. What he can be when his nature is inflamed into insurrection, has been seen in history which has been acted within our own recollection. The better side of his character exhibits him as patient and industrious, far from morose or savage, and reposing a species of religious faith in his Emperor, whom the serfs have been taught, not unsuccessfully, to regard as their real and true friend. As to the characteristic of the serf, as regards the relation of the sexes, I cannot discover much that deserves commendation. The marriage tie sits lightly enough; but the serf not unfrequently forms an intensely strong attachment, and deeply resents any interference with its object. But its impression is said not to be durable. In order to elucidate this part of the serf's character,

I have put to members of that class a variety of inquiries which might, by less scrupulous people, have been deemed a little impertinent, but which have not, so far as I could learn, caused any particular offence in the quarters where they were made. In one case, a tall handsome-looking serf, of about five and thirty, whose beard and mustache gave to his broad, good-natured face a very picturesque expression, unhesitatingly admitted that he was as successful in his love affairs, in any portion of his neighbourhood, as he could desire to be, and on his proceeding to mention his wife, my companion intimated that, of course, she was unaware of his conduct. But in reply he gave us to understand, with an air of total unconcern, that his wife was at perfect liberty to please herself in every thing not expressly connected with his personal comforts. But one glance into the interior of a serf's cottage will instantly account for any depreciation in the standard of morals. In the single room is the family altar, the stove. Upon, and against, and around that, through the long nights, are clustered, and heaped, and huddled, father, mother, brothers, sisters, relatives of all ages, without the slightest distinction. The married couple, the marriageable girls, the children, the young men growing into manhood, all are crowded together about the only means of defence against the intensity of the cold. This mode of living, recognized as one of the most fruitful sources of profligacy in England, is in Russia a habit with the mass of the peasantry.

In the event of the serf becoming utterly unable to maintain himself, or in the case of the family of the serf who is seized for the purposes of the army, the lord takes charge of the individuals reduced to this condition of helplessness. The mode in which this is managed varies; but the most ordinary is for the lord to summon certain of the other serfs around him, and commit the pauperized individuals to their charge, making such compensating arrangement as he pleases. Thus the serf is not absolutely hopeless as regards his old age or poverty; but it is stated to me that a serf can live—that is, exist—upon so little, and his powers of endurance are so considerable, that, except in cases of downright disabling, accident, or disease, the poor creatures often manage to struggle on, with such miserable volunteer assistance as they can obtain from others.

But although I have not described the ordinary condition of the serf as very flourishing, inasmuch as I have dealt with the situation of the millions rather than of the units, it must not be supposed that even among the agricultural serfs there are no exceptions. With the advantages which the serf has—his *deciatine* of fertile land, and his economical habits of living—it is almost surprising that more do not save money. And, but for the national vice of drunkenness, it is probable that great numbers of these peasants would be in a far better condition. But the moment a serf becomes the possessor of money he hurries to the drinking-house, and in a brief time the high-priced liquid in which he chiefly delights has not only drowned his reason, but emptied his pockets. There are, however, exceptions, and without adverting to cases in which serfs have acquired really large fortunes (cases not altogether so rare as might be deemed likely), I should mention that there are numerous cases in every province, of men who have been enabled to add land to land, have greatly increased their orignial stock · of farming implements, have multiplied their bullocks, and have, in fact, " prospered." Such men might be the founders of a race of yeomanry, if other times should come. It is exceedingly rare, however, for even these men to purchase their freedom. The lord, in the first place, is disinclined to lose men of that stamp from off his property, and will probably, if asked to put a value upon their freedom, name one which, however complimentary to their intrinsic worth, is effectual as an obstacle to their acquiring liberty. In the next place freedom is not the object of the aspirations of the agricultural peasant. It would place him under serious disadvantages as compared with his neighbours, and it would simply isolate without elevating him. He does not feel the common bond in which all around him are equally linked with himself a disgrace; but he feels that, by throwing it from him, he should expose himself to new burdens which might be less easily borne than the old. Freedom, which might be a boon to the serf who is a workman, and who desires liberty to journey, is not so attractive in the eyes of the agriculturist.

It is of course an item in the account of the freedom of an individual, to ascertain how far he has a remedy against those who wrong him. The serf's position in this respect is determined with no great difficulty. In the event of his lord wronging him, except in cases provided for by the law, to which reference has already been made, the serf is without redress, his lord being absolute. To suppose that the serf could get one of his master's neighbours and equals to listen to an appeal—to suppose that such neighbour should care to go out of his way to intercede for the complainant with the proprietor—and to suppose, further, that this last should not be exasperated at the slave's impertinence, and should not order him to be flogged for the same, but should redress his wrong—is one of those wild trains of improbabilities which would certainly be thought bold if employed by the writer of a Russian romance. Of the chance of such a course being conducted to a happy termination out of romance, every one may form an idea. An accident which might apprise the governor of the province of some terrible hardship inflicted on a serf might occur; and it is probable that if it did, the governor, acting in accordance with the spirit of his instructions, might proceed to order an investigation. It would then be the lord's duty, as matter of self-preservation, to see that the inquiry came to nothing. The governor is a man of rank, and wealth, and high character, and unapproachable by unworthy means; but between that official and the serf is many an individual whom none of these terms would precisely describe. The lord's rubles will do him good service, and it will be his fault if, by the time the matter again comes before the honourable officer at the head of the affairs of the locality, the whole business be not so perplexed, so distorted, and so misstated—if hostile evidence be not so suppressed, documents lost, of course by accident, and the entire case so very helpless on the side of the complainant—that little can be made of it, and it is either decided against the latter, or a series of weary delays commences, against which it is useless to appeal. If the complaint, however, arise out of an.

infraction of the " Inventory," there may be even less chance of
redress, inasmuch as the details of carrying that measure into
execution rest in hands even more accessible. As a general
rule, it may be said that the lord does not often commit injustice
in the ordinary relations between himself and his serf; but that
upon other points he does pretty much as seems good to him,
and that, practically, the serf has no available redress. And if
it be remarked that such species of interference with the pre-
carious justice of the tribunals as has been alluded to, be that of
which a high-spirited and honourable man would scruple to
avail himself, it is unfortunately necessary to reply, that—although, in their relations with their equals, the majority of
the Russian landowners would probably show themselves as
scrupulous as the ordinary rules of civilised life demand that a
gentleman should be—the whole course and current of justice
has been so polluted by the system in fatal practice in the
country, that the most notorious tampering with officials is
considered the necessary line of self-defence. But even were it
not the custom to administer bribes, wherever bribes will be
taken—that is to say, in nineteen places out of twenty—another
feeling would arise, the question being between a lord and a serf,
which would, in the mind of the former, necessitate his victory
at any price. It might be difficult to over-estimate the effect
of the precedent which would be held out to the population of
an estate by a serf's triumph over his owner.

The grave question of the state of feeling between the serf and
the lord, is not one which can be omitted from our consideration.
It is one which can only be looked at, however, in a general
light, and perhaps the exceptions on both sides run into greater
extremes than any of the phenomena of Russian life. That
instances are known in which the most deadly hostility exists
on the part of the serfs towards their lord, and that, in other
instances, similar hostility has actually broken out in the most
frightful violence is perfectly true; and, despite the almost preternatural secresy in which the occurrences of actual life here
are shrouded from the public, I am able, in reference to the
latter class of instances, to mention names and places. But, in

opposition to these terrible stories, I can also point out estates
where the lord and his family are all but idolized by their serfs;
who fly to them for advice in trouble, for charity in need, and
for medicine in sickness, and would, in return, perform any
service which the prudence, or even imprudence, of their
owner might require. But the mass of estates would appear to
be held upon a somewhat more moderate tenure of hate or love.
The serfs would not use violence to their owner, but neither
would they use it for him. They have no tie beyond that of
neighbourhood. There is none of that personal knowledge,
which gives to the intercourse of an English landed proprietor
with his tenants and poor neighbours, something of a feudal
character. The lord is probably of a different race, and of a
different creed from that of the serf. He sees nothing in his
" property" but a good or a bad investment; while the " property" can see little in the lord but a gentleman who wishes to
get rich as speedily as may be. Of a real sense of reciprocal duties there appears, as a rule, to be very little. Natural kindness
of disposition on the part of the lord, may go a long way towards
supplying the want of a better system; but it is the vicious
absence of the honourable relations between a landowner and
a land cultivator, that must perpetually render a well-managed
serf-estate an exception, and must make still more exceptional
the occurrence of those feelings between lord and serf, which it
would be most pleasant to believe in, and most agreeable to describe. I have already indicated where, as regards a superior,
whatever there is of loyalty and attachment in the serf is
directed—and there alone, in an emergency, might their sentiments be relied upon; although, brutally ignorant and terribly
debased, the serf, aroused to any manifestation of feeling, might
be a worse ally than the army of Porus found its wounded ele-
phants. Assuredly, so far as I have been successful in prosecut-
ing that part of my inquiry which refers to the feelings and
opinions of the agricultural serf, I have arrived at no indications
that he entertains, or that the lord believes him to entertain,
any great sympathy with his proprietor. Of his proprietor's
feeling towards him it is far more difficult to speak; because,

though we reduce our inquiry to a comparatively small number of objects, each has an individual character. You cannot mass a collection of educated men as you mass a horde of serfs. My own experience of these gentlemen would induce me to believe, that although they are disposed, theoretically, to take the same view upon the subject of the serf population as that entertained by the majority of disinterested persons, they are so keenly alive to the almost anomalous position they occupy, that they would give conscientious opposition to almost any experiment which should have for its object a real modification of the present system. They are content to believe that the serf, if he has his grievances, is in many respects better placed than thousands who would revolt at the name of serfdom, and that the provinces he inhabits are administered, all things considered, as fairly as they can be " with safety." They do not look for any affection or loyalty from the serf; but they think that, if let alone, and especially if let alone by the higher powers, he will continue to work out his time and theirs. And perhaps this is as much as can be expected—a humane concurrence in philanthropic theories, and in the mean time a decided resolution to "let things be."

I should here mention that the taxation of the serf population of Russia is a capitation tax, which is levied upon every male in a family, The tax is, in the first instance, collected from the serf himself by the proper officer; but, in the event of his being utterly unable to pay it, the lord becomes responsible to the Goverment. That it is at this moment in arrear to a very large amount is well known; and, indeed, the fact is candidly admitted in a paper which has been permitted to appear, and which has just been placed in my hands. The writer (whose essay is transferred to the columns of the Government journal of St. Petersburg) says, " *Les arrérages considérables d'impôts de la classe agricole servent de preuve que sa situation ne repond pas point à ses besoins.*" But long before the final appeal is made to the lord for the arrears his serfs have been unable to pay, every species of means is resorted to in order to wring the amount out of the unhappy agriculturist. Among the severest of these means—and one which I am told sometimes extorts from the suffering peasant little hoards which had been intended for the support of his age—is the plan of extinguishing the cottage stove, and so building up the chimney that the fire cannot be again lighted without suffocating the inmates of the house.   What this deprivation of warmth to a miserable family must be in the pitiless weather of Russia, I need not say; but if this *peine forte et dure* fails of its effect, I believe the hope of obtaining money in that quarter is considered at an end.   There are various hardships in the way in which this capitation tax is levied. For instance, it is affixed subject to a revision which does not occur within the interval of several years.   The tax is laid upon the number of males shown to be in the serf's family at the time it is levied.   If two-thirds or three-fourths of them are next year swept away by the cholera, as has been the case in thousands of families, the law, or rather the collector, can take no cognizance of the fact; and the serf must continue to be charged with, and if he can to pay, the same amount for the sons or brothers who have been destroyed, as he would have done in the event of their having lived, and until the next revision comes round he cannot be relieved of the absurd overcharge.

I described in an earlier chapter the condition of the serf who obtains leave of his lord to travel, and who remits to him such payment as may have been agreed upon in exchange for that liberty.   There is also an ordinary arrangement entered into between the agricultural serf and his lord, which has the same character about it.   The serf may desire to have all his time to himself, finding the land which he is occupying sufficiently profitable to deserve all his exertions.   Or he may be desirous to undertake work at a distance from his lord's estate, an offer having perhaps been made by a neighbouring landowner for a large temporary supply of labour.   In this case he bargains with the lord for a remission of the labour which he is bound to give, and stipulates for the payment of a certain sum, called the *obrok*, in lieu of it.   This arrangement is not an infrequent one; but it can, of course, be carried into effect only, or chiefly, upon well-populated estates, where the landowner can afford to dispense with the service of some of his vassals.

The condition of the Crown serf, as compared with that of the serf who belongs to a private individual, will naturally excite question. At the first glance, it would reasonably be considered that the Crown serf—held directly by the father of his people, and in whose case gain to his owner would be a secondary, or at all events not the single, object sought for—must be better situated than the individual out of whose labour it is simply the object of a grasping master to enrich himself. And so, indeed, would the case be, could any thing be done in this country in conformity with the rules of honesty. Were the Crown serfs in the condition in which the Emperor desires to see them, they would have little to complain of beyond their want of freedom. But, unhappily, the bureau system comes in between these people and the humanity of their master, and, by its shameless and grinding tyranny, places them in a worse position than their fellows. They are exposed to all the exactions and rogueries of the *employés*, and, in proportion as they appear to be nearer the fountain of justice, the more impossible it is for them to partake of its benefits. The administration which deals with these men, is perhaps as thoroughly detested as any in all Russia. The best proof that can be afforded that the nominal protection of the Crown is not even so available as the dubious security afforded by selfishness in protecting " its own," is to be found in the fact, that the number of the Crown serfs is shown by the census to be diminishing, while that of the serfs on private estates is upon the increase. The Crown serfs are taxed in the same way as the private serfs; but the rigidity with which the impost is enforced by the officials, is said to be far more severe than that displayed in the case of the private serf. The wits of the *employé*, sharpened by greediness, are constantly on the alert to see that the wretched peasant does not evade his taxation; and it is needless to say, that where a private lord would have an interest in showing forbearance, and even extending support to a good and useful serf, the official can feel nothing of the kind. The unanimous verdict appears to be, that taking into consideration the hardships to which the Crown serf is exposed, by his being brought into contact, not with an interested proprietor, but with grasping officials, his condition is less enviable than that of the agricultural peasant in private hands. There is little or no other difference in their conditions or occupations; and the description which has been given of the home and habits of the private serf, will apply to the case of the serf of the Crown.

Hitherto we have spoken only of the serf where he is grouped with a mass of individuals in similar circumstances with his own. And, as regards the agricultural serf, he must usually so be considered, as the smallest Russian estate, worth cultivating at all, requires a large number of hands upon it. It should, however, be mentioned, that there are owners of a very small number of serfs; and, though these are chiefly residents in towns, it is not so in all instances. In the case where the number is much reduced, the condition of the serf becomes proportionately worse, as he comes more constantly under the eye of his owner; while that owner is of a class which knows less shame in its avarice, than is usually found in the higher order of proprietary. Heaven help the serf whose lord, or owner, has but scant means, and has not many vassals among whom to divide his attentions! The petty and constant tyranny exercised in these cases, is said to be far worse than that displayed towards either of the classes whose conditions we have examined.

I have spoken of the serf as an uneducated being, and I have used the word advisedly, although there is a qualification which I must append to the description. He is not literally without a certain instruction, which sounds as if it were valuable, and which of course has its utility, even under the disadvantageous circumstances of the peasant. Schools have been established by government, in a great number of the country districts, expressly for the benefit of the serf; and in these schools, which are conducted upon a military system, the peasant is taught to read the Russian language, and to write. A limited portion of arithmetic is also administered, and that there may be the less wanting to make the educational course look well upon paper, a species of history—that of Russia—is included in the list of school-books. So far, therefore, as the man can be benefited by the acquirements I have mentioned in a country like this, the serf has reason to be thankful. But this reading and writing, the earlier rules of arithmetic, and the so-called history, are all, literally all, that is comprised in the peasant's education. Of real culture, of even the humblest kind, he is utterly deprived. He stands like a soldier to have the required lesson drilled into him, but nothing is added to it. Of moral training, of the humblest kind, none is given; and, of course, it is not to be expected that any instruction should be afforded likely to awaken in his mind the idea, that any other duties can be demanded of a man than hard work and fidelity to his Sovereign. It may be said that, having been taught to read, he is enabled to acquire moral and secular information for himself; and this would be a just argument in a different country—in France, for example, or England. But in Russia you have done little for the man whom you have only taught to read Russian. The religious works used by his Church are in Sclavonic, and consequently he peruses them as an uneducated Roman Catholic reads Latin—that is to say, the words are on his lips, but they convey no idea to his mind. And he has no other books to which he can gain acess. There is no publication of works of any value to him, in the only language he can comprehend, and if there were he could not obtain them. Virtually he is as much excluded from the sources of knowledge as if he had not been taught at all; and that this is not mere surmise, may be seen in the helpless and brutal ignorance of many a man into whose hands, if you put a Russian book, he will read it to you with an ease which would delight a " visiting committee." The absence of the moral sense, which would be produced by the simplest and humblest form of training, is too painfully evident to need pointing out; the degradation of mind and of morals is equal, but in the mockery of tuition, such as is afforded in the schools I speak of, the government finds an excuse for doing nothing better, and—which is more valuable to it—a justification for a boast to Europe that the Russian peasant is an educated man. It is very desirable that this system should be thoroughly understood before any hypothesis is reared upon the fact that there is a great deal of schooling in Russia. It would be worse than imprudent to assume, from the returns of scholars at these establishments, that the mass of population among whom they have been planted, have been thereby brought one inch nearer the condition which might justify their rulers in entrusting them with privileges. On the contrary, there could perhaps be no greater danger to civilisation, than the attempting to excite these men to any demonstration in behalf of civil rights. The Russian would, in the first place, blindly believe whatever representation was made to him, and would rush to the fulfilment of his new-acquired idea with the dogged energy of the savage; at the first check, hesitation, or hindrance in his way, his own untaught and untrained nature would blaze out, and we have seen the results already, in deeds almost too dreadful to be written. No, the peasant has little to be thankful for in the education which has been given him—its best fruits are, that it enables him to hold his own a little better when a squabble upon money matters arises between him and his superior, and that his national character, such as it is, has been confirmed, and his devotion to his original habits and customs strengthened, by the historical course of reading he has gone through; for the history of Russia which has been imparted to him is framed upon the safest possible principle—that of proving the country in which he lives to be the noblest, wisest, most prosperous, most religious, and most civilized nation in the world, and the only one governed in a way really approved by Divine Providence.

The whole of the present chapter has been devoted to the condition of the serf; and, if the subject has necessitated a somewhat dry and matter-of-fact mode of treatment, I trust that I shall be pardoned for having dwelt thus upon a topic which will, one of these days, be "the question" in Russia. I might have reduced into somewhat livelier form my notes of visits to the dwellings of these people; and assuredly the artist who has an eye for the grotesque, whether he labour with pen or with pencil, has the richest field for his talent among the lower classes of Russia. As regards personal appearance, there is every conceivable variety of startling quaintness and ugliness. Among the older women, squatted by their stoves, or sunning themselves at the doorstep, I have seen scores of faces into which the accumulated hideousness of a hundred nightmares would seem to have been crowded for the dismay of beholders. What visions I have beheld of these old women, some of them crippled or shrunken as regarded their bodies, but with vast heads and masculine features of enormous size, which, amid the deep wrinkles and the white bristly hairs upon the face, gave the idea of great and cruel strength. Sometimes, getting among them, where I have found a group clustered together of all ages, from the terrible hags I speak of, whose years no one might think of counting, down to the tiniest and ugliest babes (the Russian babies are very ugly), swathed and rigid, I have half-realised a picture which I saw in one of the Continental galleries, in which the mad whims of a middle-age painter have broken out in a large scene describing the horrors of hell. In the appallingly ridiculous faces of that "sick man's dream," where huge heads of great viciousness are walking about bodiless, but sustained by naked splay feet growing from their necks—where other faces grin at you from lurking-places at the end of some filthy abyss of impossible perspective—and others again, like ghouls, are perching on the bodies of the damned, and either scratching out their eyes with hot rakes, or making a horrid feast out of the more sensitive parts of the system,—I have scarcely seen more hideousness than I have seen indicated, and ready for a painter's development into actual terrorism, among these lower class serfs. I could not have believed in such living caricatures of the image of divinity. Hitherto I have often wondered where many of the old masters could have obtained the revolting originals of their hags and fiends; but I can now understand that a painter, in a morbid state of mind, might stray away from the haunts of civilised beings, and plunging into the country, might make his way to some old, squalid, dreary village, where, among living and breathing Troglodytes, or such creatures as those I have seen, he might fill his mind with shapes of savage deformity. I have certainly seen Anglo-Saxons ugly enough; but I never witnessed in England the type of so much grimness. There are remarkable Jews

I

here, too, of fearful age, and whose miserable dress, long grizzled beards, and glittering eyes, would be a fortune to an artist. Their intense eagerness, their clutching with their long, dirty, bony hands, and the preternatural volubility with which they hurry out a jargon known only to themselves, are all characterized by an intensity to which the energy of their brethren. among us is a mere nothing. They linger about in front of a coffee-house appropriated to them here; and as a victim comes, out flies the lean arm and clutches him, drawing him close, that the old man's mouth may reach his ear—one thinks of the frightful Polypus, seen by the diver (in Schiller's ballad), at the bottom of the gulf. But the artist's sketch-book need not be entirely filled with ugly faces and shapeless forms. Among the serf girls he will find many a countenance and limb which will help him with his nymphs and rustics. The expression in the faces of many of these girls is confiding and child-like, and is frequently aided by very delicate features, and by blue eyes of much softness. They are tall, and walk with a swinging step, and, being little encumbered by drapery, they get over the ground at a capital pace. How they manage to exist with so few clothes is a mystery—the male serf is well wrapped up, and seems to take care of himself; but the girls appear to have as little upon them as possible, and what they have is of the thinnest and scantiest kind. On a wet day—and I have seen some days when the rain came down with deluging impetuosity—I have observed the peasant girl, throwing her exceedingly thin frock over her head, and thereby rendering it painfully evident to the most discreet observer, that the dingy petticoat below was companionless, trudge about in the teeth of a cutting wind, and, meeting a friend, stand chattering and laughing for an hour, with no more apparent consciousness of the bitter weather around her than if the day were brilliancy itself. The hardihood and cheerfulness of these girls are very remarkable; they carry weights obviously too great for their strength with great willingness for long distances, and they sing all the way, except when the song is interrupted for a jest with a friend, or a good-natured greeting to the stranger. They marry, unluckily, very young, and have swarms of children, and then, although it is melancholy to think of it, some of those whose bright eyes and merry laugh have set rival suitors beating one another's thick skulls, and rending one another's huge beards, become in process of years the hideous old women who seem to have been created only for the use of artists. It would have been easy, and by no means unpleasant, to have enlivened my observations upon serf life with sketches from the houses into which I have been, or of the groups continually to be met in the streets and country; but I thought it better to confine myself for the moment to the details of a social system, which not only presents a very grave aspect to the philanthropist of to-day, but may afford a very grave problem for the statesman of to-morrow.

CHAPTER VII.

THE next province to which I will advert is Bessarabia.

This district is essentially different, in most important respects, from the rich corn provinces to which attention has already been given. Its history is not theirs. It is the fruit of comparatively recent military successes obtained over a neighbour. Bessarabia, formerly part of Moldavia, was formally surrendered by Turkey to Russia in 1812, a cession including all that part of Moldavia which lies to the east of the river Pruth. It were unjust to deprive that boundary stream of its dignity; but having seen the important division line on my way to Odessa, I am compelled to confess that a brook would be a designation more nearly consonant with the result of one's own observation. Bessarabia's more imposing boundaries are the Danube and the Dniester, between which it lies.

Thus acquired, Bessarabia was not found to be inhabited by a class similar to that which, as we have seen, constitutes the agricultural population of the great corn provinces. It had no lower nation of serfs ready to be affixed to allotted soil. Great numbers of its inhabitants appear to have fled. It is certain that the newly gained district was by no means populated to an extent which could render it valuable to its fresh masters, and it became necessary to encourage, either directly or indirectly, an influx of labour and productive power. The government, therefore, saw fit to allow almost any body who chose it to settle in Bessarabia, with little or no questioning as to whence he had come, or whether he were his own property or any body else's, and he often obtained an allotment of land, and soon became established in the province. I am informed that this attraction drew away great numbers of serfs from other parts of the Russian dominions. I referred to this fact in a former chapter, when alluding to the condition of certain slaves who had effected their escape. The result was to people Bessarabia, although by no means to the full; and the population, as may easily be surmised, is of a very mixed character, and, were pedigrees traced, would be found to contain representatives of almost every department of the empire. Bessarabia is not one of the great corn provinces of Russia. The vocation of its inhabitants is chiefly the breeding of cattle and sheep. There is a cultivation of Indian corn to a considerable extent, but it is principally used as the food for the people themselves ; very little of it finds its way to the Odessa market, except under the pressure of some extraordinary stimulus of famine prices. In regard to corn, therefore, this province need not be taken into the general account. Its pasturages are rich and extensive, and cattle from considerable distances are sent thither for grazing.

Large estates in Bessarabia are in the hands of individuals high in office and honour in the Russian empire. Count Nesselrode, for example, has a fine estate there, comprising, perhaps, 50,000 deciatines, and other noblemen, whose names are well known in Europe, are among the Bessarabian landlords. Much of the information which I have obtained in reference to this province has been afforded me through the kindness of a proprietor of one of its estates, who has had the opportunity of comparing the condition of his own district with that of other countries, and whose opinions are entitled, therefore, to a degree of attention which might not be due to one who had possessed more limited facilities of observation. I do not know that I can do better than give the substance of his own words :—

" The species of test to which you would submit the agricultural districts of Russia, presupposes a system. You would take it for granted that the Russian farmer goes to work like a man of business, and as his contemporary in England or Scotland would do—carefully considering his whole plan of operations, keeping such accounts as will enable him at any period to compare their successes, and prepared to adopt such alterations, and to make such fresh combinations, as his books, and the state of his farm, may dictate. Such is not the course of the Russian farmer. He has no system, unless that may be called one which consists in an implicit reliance on the wisdom of those who have preceded him, and even in the precedents of his own customs. The Russian farmer, in effect, is in a state nearer akin to that of barbarism than the majority of his fellow-subjects—I speak of barbarism, of course, in a qualified sense, and as signifying what is in arrear of the advances of civilisation and science. And as regards ordinary registers of agricultural operation, such as those you have in England, the Russian knows nothing of them. Certain rude records in the shape of accounts are kept upon most farms; but as for the system which teaches the English or Scotch farmer to keep books like those of the trader, and enables him to show balance-sheets at the end of his term, it is certainly foreign to the Russian's ideas either of utility or practicability. I use a familiar expression when I say that a Russian ' gets on ' as well as he can, but how he gets on is hardly known to himself or to any body else.

" Therefore, of course, if you ask me to state what are the farmer's ideas of capital, of remunerative price, and of safe or unsafe investment, I am unable to answer you, and I am quite certain that he himself would be even more puzzled to reply. If you inquire all over Russia as to the real amount of produce in the various districts, you will receive the most contradictory, and often the most absurd, answers. For example, you will be told, in reference to the sowing of corn and the harvest, ' that ten for one' is produced—a boast which has been made, and which has sounded formidably in the ears of Europe, but which I know to be utter nonsense. But another farmer to whom you may apply is just as likely to tell you that ' two for one' is the average product, which is an enormous under-rating, except in a very bad year. If I were asked the question, I should answer, though not with certainty, that about ' six for one,' including all kinds of corn, might be about the mark in an average year. But I do not believe there exist at this moment materials in Russia which could enable an inquirer to make up the account of the harvest whose products are now before your eyes, on their way to the ships.

" And as regards Bessarabia, in which I am more immediately interested, although it is not a great corn country, it seems to have adopted the want of system characteristic of the corn provinces. I do not suppose that even the omnipotent order of the Emperor could elicit a really valuable return, one worthy to be ranked among agricultural statistics, although, upon such an emergency as that, something would of course be framed which would answer the purpose of the authorities. I could tell you what is done on my own estate, but you must not suppose that my neighbours, right and left, would recognise that as their guide, or that they would confirm me as to the majority of the details I could give you. You could not with safety assert the existence of any system from what I should describe. But I will mention in the first place a few points upon which there would be, and could be, no diversity of information.

" You inquire about taxes. Well, we have no taxes. That sounds pleasantly, does it not? No, we have no taxes, except a small local tax, which is said to be for the maintenance of roads, an outlay of no great magnitude, and a subject upon which, as you know, we are not very anxious. There is, however, a payment which perhaps may be considered in the light of a tax, except that it is voluntary with the inhabitant whether he will pay it or not. This is the sum paid to Government for exempting us from having soldiers quartered upon us, a proceeding which is much followed in the free districts of Russia. In connection with this is a point worth mentioning, as it illustrates the wise and careful system of administration pursued in this country. The exemption amount is charged upon the value of the property inhabited. To show how Government is treated, it is only necessary to say that whereas, for the purposes of regulating this exemption, property is valued at an amount ridiculously below the real value, the contractor who has to give security to Government for the due fulfilment of his contract, and who either assigns property of his own—or, more commonly, procures security from other persons, at an average rate of four per cent. interest—usually contrives to have such property estimated at three times its value, at least. There is no real rule for such valuations, except that which is made convenient to certain functionaries to adopt; for the house in which you are sitting"—(I can give a London reader an idea of the size of the house, which is situated in the neighbourhood of Odessa, by saying that it resembled one of the best class of villas in the Hampstead-road)—"about five pounds a year is paid for the exemption from liability to give quarters to the soldiery.

" The payment, as I have said, is not necessary, and, in the case of the humbler population, it is not usual. The Government treats the free peasant here as if he were a conquered subject, and *vœ victis!* The poor agriculturist is ruined by the imposition of this burden, from which the serf is protected; for I need hardly say that it is not the interest of a lord that his slave should be beggared by having to provide for the soldier. Nor, were the law adhered to, would the imposition itself be so inordinately oppressive, although, under any circumstances, it would be heavy. By law, all that the peasant has to find for the soldier quartered upon him is firing, quarters, and salt. But, practically, the soldier lives upon the unfortunate peasant. As for any appeal upon the subject in a nation where the army is looked upon as the ' one thing needful,' and is favoured in every possible way, that is out of the question for a man who has scarcely the means of living, far less of bribing the officials in whose hands is the administration of law. I do not accuse the military authorities of any desire to be oppressive; on the contrary, I say, without hesitation, that the only quarter in which one can look in Russia with any hope of success, for a manifestation of an effort to be just and humane, is in the superior grades of the Russian army; but it is not to be expected that, under the circumstances, they should be disposed to concede any advantages, or to seek a limitation of the soldier's claims. It is simply a notorious fact, that the peasant in whose house the soldier is quartered keeps him. The cost of the large bodies of military in the district of which I am speaking, is thus heavily thrown upon the class least able to bear it; but it must be added, such is the system that there is nothing saved to the Government by reason of the amount in which the peasant is

amerced above that prescribed by law. The Government itself
is charged with the extra provision for the soldier's living, and,
wearied as an inquirer into Russian life must be with the constant iteration of the subject, I must point out that jobbery and
corruption here find another harvest.

"And now as regards our produce. I believe you are aware
that the question which has in recent years engaged the attention of such of our agriculturists as have eyes for any thing about
them, has been the breeding of the Merino sheep, and the problem to be solved has been, whether the expense and risk of
breeding these animals will be compensated for by the profits.
The experiment has been tried upon a large and a small scale,
and is still pursued, although some proprietors have given it up
in despair. There are cases of landowners possessing as many
as 50,000 and even 90,000 sheep. And so valuable are certain
of these animals that in a *troupeau d'élite*, as we term it, which
was purchased a short time ago for a nobleman, and which consisted only of sheep of pure blood, one ram of exceeding beauty
and vigour, was valued and paid for at the price of £40—of
course a case of rare exception. But the chief portion of these
sheep are half-bred, and yield what is called metis wool, which
may fairly take rank with that produced in your Australian
colonies. The manufacturer has his choice between the 'long
staple,' which of course takes the lead as regards quantity, and
the 'fine staple,' the quality of which is its characteristic. As
I do not myself breed these sheep, I have been spared the
anxiety attendant upon the solution of the problem of profit;
but, from being acquainted with numbers of sheep-breeders,
both large and small, and having had frequent occasion to watch
the progress of their experiments, from the first purchase of stock
up to the present time, I may claim a better acquaintance with
the general question, than perhaps an individual proprietor
might possess. There are scarcely two of them with whom I am
intimate, who pursue precisely the same course with their sheep;
but I find that an accident, or disease incident to some particular
year, easily turns many of these individuals from a plan which
they had previously declared could be the only rational one,

from which it is fair to argue that they have often proceeded
upon hastily formed notions. But there is one result to which,
as it appears to me, all these experiments will come, sooner or
later, although it may be many years before those who have
taken so enthusiastically to sheep-breeding will confess to its
not being suited to Russia. Our climate stands in the way of
our profit. Our merinoes flourish, and the wool is excellent,
and commands its price in every market where wool is known.
But the great number of months during which it is impossible
to allow the sheep to graze, during which house accommodation
must be afforded them, and house food must also be given them,
will always prevent us from maintaining a successful competition with those who may be enabled to add to all the advantages
of our breed a climate which will, generally speaking, enable the
sheep to dispense with artificial protection; and to revert to
what I have already referred to, as Russians become better and
more precise book-keepers, they will generally discover what
many among them have already found out, namely, that the
conditions of success in merino breeding are wanting to our
country. But I do not anticipate this discovery being made at
a very early period.

"As regards cattle, the breeding of that class of animal is liable,
generally speaking, to only the ordinary risks of a pursuit which
is tolerably well understood among us. But the frightful ravages
of the last distemper, in which it has been estimated that a mil-
lion head of cattle must have perished, would be looked upon
as an accident which we have a right to hope may not recur.
Its effect has been to raise the price, especially of the oxen used
for the purposes of draught, and of the cow. I can answer your
inquiries as to prices, by averages which, upon inquiry, you will
find confirmed pretty generally. The price of a bullock, such as
is used for drawing, ranges during seasons where no such epide-
mic prevails, from 18 silver rubles to 30; and, perhaps a bullock
which has been accustomed to draw, will, if sold with his usual
comrade, fetch a couple of rubles additional. The price of a milk
cow ranges from 40 to 60 rubles, and a calf of six to seven
months old, should fetch fifteen rubles. But to estimate the

real value of these animals, it is necessary to know the real cost of their food and of their produce. The following may be taken as a fair average account of the price of the articles mentioned, when sold in the south of Russia. Hay, by the load (that of two bullocks), about six silver rubles, and extreme periods have occurred, when it has mounted up to twenty rubles. Straw, sixty trusses (but these are about half the size of the ordinary English truss), a ruble and a half. Great quantities of straw are purchased simply as fuel, for which purpose it is largely used. On the other hand, the price of milk is about thirteen kopecs silver per quart."

It seems to me well to add here the prices of a variety of other articles, the result either of agricultural labour, or otherwise connected with the land. I have taken considerable pains to verify these by repeated inquiries, and they may be depended on. They refer, of course, to the ordinary market prices in the south of Russia. Beef, three silver kopecs per pound—containing ten per cent. less than our own pound. Mutton, about the same. Veal, six silver kopecs. Bread, six silver kopecs per pound. The best white wheaten, twenty silver kopecs. Fresh butter, twenty-three silver kopecs. Salt butter, seven silver rubles per *pood.* Eggs, ten silver kopecs for ten. Of cheese so little is made that it cannot be included among the ordinary agricultural products. As regards poultry, I find that a turkey, not fattened, will usually cost a silver ruble, and a pair of fowls about forty silver kopecs. And for fuel, wood is sold by the cubic fathom, but the packing is so bad that it is difficult to say how much is included in that admeasurement—such nominal fathom is, however, about twenty-three rubles, and charcoal is one silver ruble per chetwert. And, in further reference to bread, for the information of those who may wish to compare the Russian peasant's loaf with that of the English labourer, I will add that rye bread may be estimated at one English penny per English pound, and coarse wheaten brown bread at the same price. And the average wages of a good labourer range from twenty-five to thirty kopecs silver a day, and in and near towns often rise to forty.

I will now illustrate another chapter in the Russian system. I have recorded the statement of my most intelligent informant, who, in speaking of the free districts of Russia, remarked that there were "no taxes." My next reference will be to the working of a system which is substituted over all the country for an excise duty. We shall see how far a nominal exemption in this respect, and a rigid monopoly, work, as regards the interest of the Government and of the people.

You are travelling—it may be in your carriage, if you happen to have a strong faith in its powers of endurance—and you observe your driver look wistfully at a wretched kind of large hovel situate at the junction of a couple of the paths which, by a strange misuse of language, are called roads in Russia. You call to him to know what the place in question is, and he replies to you in Russian—the material word of his answer being *katchma*. He has already checked the horses— so, as you begin to perceive that the place is a species of inn, you signify that he may halt. You find that you have stopped at a shed or covered yard, looking into which, you will observe filth of every description, and possibly some oxen, looking moodily round at you from their hay, or a miserable horse or two, much too hopeless to give the ordinary greeting with which a horse that is in the habit of being well fed salutes you when you enter his stable. To the right and left of this shed you see an appearance of a lodge for human habitation, and if you push open a door on the left, you will see a batch of Russian clowns, and among them a carrier or two, who are drinking brandy, and bawling out songs of extreme vigour, both as regards the music and the sentiment. They will honour you with a stare, but will not pay any other attention, unless you happen to be in uniform; and a remarkably villanous-looking Jew will waddle from behind a sort of screen, and, according to his frame of mind, will either offer you a stool, or ask you what you want there. Look at him, with his grizzled beard, keen black eye, and long, ragged, greasy coat. Wretch as he seems, he is a superior creature to the "Christians" around him, and they keep following him with their eyes, let him move where he will,

as animals will watch you as you walk round a room. Your
driver has entered behind you, having, as usual, wasted little
time in taking care of his horses. He, as your friend, advises
you to sit down, and even (the attention was shown to me during one of my excursions in Russia) spits upon his cuff to
cleanse the stool for you more delicately. He signs to the Jew,
who presently sets before you a bottle of brandy and a tumbler.
Perhaps you taste the spirit, and sicken at the odour. But you
push over the bottle and tumbler to your servant, and look
round. The grimy stove, the muddy window, a rabble of
mongrel dogs dodging about your legs, the boors stupefying
themselves, and occasionally howling out a scrap of blatant
minstrelsy, and the general aid of cold, discomfortable debauchery, fix themselves with daguerreotype rapidity and precision
upon your memory. So does the look of cunning complicity
interchanged between your driver and your host, when, having
"seen enough," you demand the price, are charged forty silver
kopecs (the price of a whole bottle of poisonous brandy), and
the driver assures you that the charge is correct. You throw
down the money, and, as a prudent traveller, you turn your
servant out before he can drink more than his tumbler full.
Vain precaution, for when the carriage is again on the road,
and he has seen you into your seat, he runs back to get the
other glass, which he has clearly earned by helping the Jew to
cheat you.

In revenge you pester him by incessantly calling to him with
cautions, and vexing his soul with questions injurious to his
reputation for good driving, or for knowledge of where he is
going. Perhaps you question him about the place he has just
left, but in that case you will not get much more out of him
than an iteration of the word *katchma*. But if he could or
would enlighten you, he would apprise you that the government
of his country enjoys a monopoly of brandy, and that it farms
out that monopoly, in slices, to individuals who are called
"brandy-farmers"—that these individuals compete by tender
for the exclusive right of selling brandy to the subjects of the
Crown and the serfs of the lord—and that even the landowner,

if he manufactures brandy, is compelled to sell it to the brandy-farmer, or rather is forbidden to sell it to any one else, except that he may vend it, retail, upon his own estate, in order to increase his income by encouraging his serfs to brutalize themselves. Some little further insight may thus be gained into the flourishing fortunes of the Russian corn-grower, when it is known—and the matter is too commonly notorious to be contested—that many estates have no clear profit whatever except that which arises from the retail sale of brandy to the peasant. The lord, who of course deputes his authority, allows a Jew to take or erect one of those sheds upon some convenient part of his estate, where the greatest number of people are likely to be passing, and there he establishes the drinking-place, the name of which, as used in the south, we have already repeated, but which is called a *kabak* in the northern part of the empire; and the Hebrew delegate of the Catholic sells to the Greek the abominable liquor in question. It is' usually made from rye; but when the wheat upon the estate does not promise to command a ready sale, or when, thanks to the admirable arrangements of roads and carriages, there is no great chance of that sale being a profitable one, the corn itself is used for the manufacture of the " fire-water."

The brandy-farmer himself is a gambler who sees strange variations of fortune, but who always clings to his play to the last possible moment. He takes a large district, at an exorbitant price, and having given security to government in the way I have already referred to, he usually finds himself getting deeper and deeper into the debt of the State year by year. But if he cannot manage to make his fortune out of one district, and has to pray indulgence for his arrears, he usually tries to have another and another annexed to it, in the hope by setting upon several cards to win on one at least. In the meantime he is generally living in unbounded luxury and extravagance, by way of increasing his chance of paying what he has undertaken to pay. But if the people will not or cannot get so drunk, or get drunk so often, as is necessary to enable him to prosper, it is not his fault; and for a long time the government appear to think, so, for arrears are allowed to accumulate to a terrible extent. It is said that in the case of some of the larger defaulters, who have of course given very extensive available security, let it be overvalued as it may, the authorities hesitate to exert their right of foreclosing, from a reluctance to take possession of the very startling quantity of property which would thus come into their hands. Every way, therefore, the system goes wrong, the nation is cheated, and, what is worse, a direct interest in producing demoralization is created among those who should be teachers and examples.

Of the provinces of which I originally spoke as forming the Russian territories on the Black Sea, we have surveyed the condition of the most important—and, indeed, it may be said, of all which bear a considerable part in the production of the agricultural wealth of Russia. But there are several circumstances connected with the remaining portions of the territories in question, which make it desirable to refer to each in its turn.

Cherson is one of those provinces which is entirely formed of Steppe land, and in which the obstacles to corn-growing have therefore proved too great for that pursuit to be the staple occupation of the inhabitants. There is but little corn grown in Cherson, and that little produces a satisfactory harvest upon rare occasions only, perhaps once in seven or eight years. At other times the inhabitants are compelled to struggle with the disadvantages of their position, and by dint of every makeshift to which a distressed agricultural class can resort, including that of payments in kind, contrive to exist, although the precariousness of their condition frequently renders it most unfortunate. I find, indeed, from a paper which has been prepared under the inspection of the Russian Government, that the opinion entertained in Russia itself of the Steppe soil, is unfavourable to the probability of its ever being cultured with advantage. It is true that in certain portions of the south we find a different system of cultivation, but one which is certainly not more scientific than that which has been described. The vast and comparatively unvalued plains of this part of the country enable the agriculturist to adopt a course which, in no other civilized land,

would be thought of, or could be practicable. This is to cultivate a certain portion of the land, get out of it whatever it is
capable of yielding, and then, instead of taking any further
trouble with it, to abandon it, and begin sowing somewhere
else. The practice may be defended on the ground that a fine
crop is seldom or never got off the Steppe, except upon virgin
soil.

But this part of the empire, though poor in corn, is rich in
cattle, which are bred for a manufacture largely carried on in
Cherson, namely, that of tallow. The three governments of
Ekaterinoslov, Tchernomori, and Worenege, are the great places
where this manufacture is pursued. The history of the tallow is
briefly this. When the animals are well fattened—that is to say,
about autumn—they are slaughtered, and the first melting takes
place, the result of which is the production of a very fine tallow,
which, however, is not so acceptable in the market as the material
in a more adulterated form. The tallow thus having undergone
the first process, is distributed into parcels of twenty poods each.
It is wrapped round with mats, and as soon as the weather sets in
cold, it is placed upon sledges, for it will not bear such wheel
carriage as the country can afford, and is sent to Bielgorod,
which is in the government of Koursk. Here it undergoes a
second melting, and the "tricks of the trade" begin here. It is put
into casks, and its price is now about eleven rubles the pood.
From this place it is sent away to the various markets. The
north of Russia has the chief part of the trade, but it is stated
that attempts are being made to divert it to Taganrog. The
system of adulteration and of gambling which is connected with
the tallow trade is not precisely within the scope of these chapters,
but it would be worth the attention of some mercantile "Lancet."

The town of Cherson, which has been called the capital of
New Russia, was built by Catherine the Second on the north
bank of the Dnieper. Its vicinity possesses its most enduring
claim to the attention of the world, from its possessing the
remains of our own John Howard, who died here, a victim to
his philanthropical zeal, in 1790. Some Russians to whom I
was speaking, adverted to the fact of his monument in Cherson

having been erected by one of themselves, and remarked that England had given herself no concern about his memory. They were surprised to hear that at all events we had given him a statue in St. Paul's—an honour which they appreciated more keenly when I informed them that the edifice was chiefly devoted to monuments to the most distinguished members of the military and naval professions.

The other province to which I will briefly advert (rather to complete the list, however, than because I can, in this case, offer the results of personal inquiry), is that of Tauris, which includes the Crimea. This, again, is not one of the agricultural districts; the character of its Steppe soil precluding its taking its place among them. The country itself has had a series of masters of different races, the Genoese having been driven from it by the Tartars in the fifteenth century; and the latter having held it as tributary to the Turks till 1774. In 1783 the Russians took possession of it, and it was formally ceded to them shortly afterwards. The upper portion of the Crimea is flat and comparatively barren, but it is among the mountains southward that the country takes another and a more delightful aspect. There the land becomes fertile, and that advantage, coupled with the beautiful mountain scenery, has induced the selection of this part of the Crimea for the country residences of distinguished personages. One of the magnificent of these residences has been erected by Prince Woronzow, at Alapka, and although duties of a still higher order than those of a nobleman upon his own estates enforce the absence of the illustrious owner, who usually holds viceregal court far away, the utmost courtesy and attention are invariably shown to any traveller, especially to an Englishman, who may desire a sight of the edifice. The graver duties of an inquiry which permitted but little time for pleasure-visits, forbade me to sacrifice the number of days which a journey to this part of the country would have demanded; and from the descriptions afforded me, by an English gentleman at Odessa, who has had opportunities of admiring the lordly terraces and noble chambers of the chateau, and of examining in detail its elaborate elegance, it must be a

K

matter of regret to me that I have been prevented from seeing this specimen of Russian magnificence, which, it should also be remarked, is the result of the architectural talent of an Englishman. The Crimea is remarkable for producing excellent fruit of various kind, and especially walnuts; and instances are not infrequent of a whole family being supported by the sale of the produce of two or three of the walnut-trees which flourish in the better portion of the peninsula. But the Crimea has other and more important features in its ports, and their connection with the naval power and purposes of Russia.

Although Azof is not strictly within the term of territories bordering upon the Black Sea, a few words upon that position of the empire may not be out of place. The Sea of Azof labours under great disadvantage in regard to temperature, and scarcely enjoys more freedom from ice than the northern parts of Russia. Were it otherwise, and were the navigation of the Don improved, this sea might become an invaluable rendezvous for foreign, and receptacle for native, produce. But the suddenness of the frosts which block up its waters for months, and the shifting and changing character of the obstacles thrown up by the Don, present in combination almost insuperable difficulties in the way of continuous commerce in the Azof. The Russian Government—probably more alive to these facts than those who would censure what has been called an " obstructive" policy in regard to the admission of foreigners into this sea—has sought to make it less a centre of commerce than " a nursery for seamen;" and though it may be questionable how far the more important part of a sailor's duty can be learned in the Azof, it may not be undesirable that attention should be given to the uses to which this *mer bien gardée* is turned by its rulers. The Don, for commercial purposes, is said to be even less available than it was in the time of Peter the Great, but there is something of his spirit moving in the Azof.

I will here terminate the inquiry to which these chapters have been chiefly devoted. A concluding chapter will comprise two or three incidents of Russian administration (as seen in the public offices of Odessa), which may give some little additional illustration of the system of which they are a part, and I shall also have one or two more pleasant recollections to record. I may, however, be permitted to state, that having started for Russia without having bestowed very much more specific study upon her internal administration than is usually given by an Englishman, I have had few preconceived notions to abandon or correct—and that, even if the topics to which I have devoted myself had not been in a great measure removed from the influence of possible prejudice, I have at least entered the Black Sea without any prepossessions on my mind. I have merely felt it my duty to obtain from those best qualified to give information, such details as seemed to me necessary to illustrate the subject, and to confirm such details by comparisons, and, wherever it was practicable, by personal investigation. The vast extent of the districts to which my attention has been directed, the absence of means of communication and of residence, and the character of the inhabitants themselves, necessarily preclude such a survey as in countries of railways, diligences, and inns, becomes the natural mode of obtaining information. My course was, first, to discover individuals from the different regions in question, and to overcome their greater or less unwillingness to afford what I sought; and, aided by the advice of gentlemen intimate with Russia and the Russians, and further assisted by my own excursions and observations in such parts of the country as were within my reach, and by my researches among the humbler and working classes on the Steppe, and in the city, I have collected a mass of notes of which these chapters contain the pith.

CHAPTER VIII.

IT is not a very easy thing to get into Russia, but it is a far more difficult one to get out of it. Russia neither

" Welcomes the coming, (nor) speeds the parting guest."

But the obstacle interposed between an outside traveller and the domains of the Emperor is of a single character. He is either allowed to enter, or he is not. There is no great array of technicalities in the case. But when you have partaken of Russian hospitality until you have spent a sufficiency of silver rubles, and desire to visit some land where prohibitory tariffs do not compel you to pay about three times the value of almost every article you buy, your endeavours to escape must be seconded by energy and pertinacity. I speak of a foreigner's case. I believe that a Russian must possess something more than even those valuable qualities before he can obtain leave to quit. But I will speak only of a stranger's position, as illustrated by my own.

When the vessel in which I arrived was moored in the harbour, a couple of Custom-house officers came on board to inspect the baggage. The scrutiny was very severe; and here, as at Orsova, books seemed to give the officials the greatest discomfort. My travelling library was very small, but, being in English, it occasioned much shaking of the head. It was amusing to see the eagerness with which the men read every word of the title-pages, in the hope of gaining some clue to the character of the contents. Sometimes, in extreme helplessness, they would consult other passengers, and then lay the books down on the seats, and take them up again after a little time, as if they expected the printing to become more legible by exposure to the air, like marking ink. Any explanations of mine were received with evident suspicion, and for a long time, I feared that my books would be carried off and impounded. But after a last and very melancholy look over them—a process pursued by each in turn, in a way which reminded me of Gurth, Robin Hood, and Wamba, when Front de Bœuf's letter is delivered to them before Torquilstowe—they decided on risking the thing, and I was allowed to repack my trunk. And as I left the vessel I was told to apply to the police for my passport next day.

The police-office is at the opposite side of Odessa from that of the harbour. It is remarkable for a somewhat lofty tower, from which a watch is kept up for fires in the town, and there are huge balls which can be hoisted as signals, variously arranged so as to indicate to the officials the quarter in which the conflagration may have broken out. The building itself is extensive. The intense respect which the inhabitants of Russia are taught to show to every thing bearing the semblance of authority, was curiously evinced by many of the persons entering with me, who uncovered their heads with great deference, long before they reached the outside door, and bowed most humbly to the scrubbiest-looking clerk they met in their way to the departments within. The same reverence, I observed, was shown at the post-office, where the persons bringing letters stood uncovered, with bated breath and whispering humbleness, as if they were imploring a great favour from the close-cropped clerks tendering the missives for despatch; and I thought how an Englishman would stare—as a prelude to an impromptu commination—if a clerk at St. Martin's-le Grand signed to him to take off his hat while handing in his letter. After wandering through a variety of rooms, in each of which I was desired to explain my business, and then, after being asked a variety of questions, was referred to another department (for there were no notifications on the doors, as in France and England, of the duties performed in each locality), I was informed that when I wanted to go away I must come *there*, but in the meantime I must apply to the governor. I should observe that the Russian authorities take it for granted that every body is to understand the Russian language, and although it is *de rigueur* to speak French in society, few of the police officials with whom I came in contact understood a word of the latter tongue. As a passport-bureau is supposed to be especially constituted for dealings with foreigners, this selection of *employés* is judiciously contrived for the stranger's confusion and discomfiture.

So much time having been wasted, thanks to the directions received on board the boat, I went off to the governor's. His Excellency's chancery is in the house which contains the public library, and looks upon Richelieu's statue, and Prince Woronzow's giant staircase. Here I found a much better class of officials, who received me with civility, and told me to come again in two or three days. Before this period had elapsed, I had the honour of making the personal acquaintance of the governor; and as at that moment I had not been made aware of the time I should lose in visiting the Crimea (from the infrequency of any communication), I requested a passport for that district, and his Excellency politely ordered one for me. I did not therefore again apply until desirous of leaving Russia, and then I found that I ought to have obtained a *billet de séjour*, and that I had been living unlawfully; but divers explanations on my part induced this informality to be overlooked.

The next thing with which I was furnished was a printed notification to the police, on the part of the governor's chancery, that I was to be taken in hand. And this, together with my passport, I was desired to take to my friends, the police. Away I went, and reached the fire-tower about mid-day. It was of no use trying to form any idea of the office to which one ought to apply—the only plan was to exhaust the capabilities of the whole establishment, by which process I trusted at last to get my work done. I tried five or six rooms, in each of which the clerks, the majority of whom were remarkably dirty, heard my application patiently, as if comprehending it, and then grinned at one another, as if intimating that it was a very fine thing not to be able to understand any language but their own. English was out of the question. French no better, and even Italian was useless. But I determined to inspect the whole establishment, and wandered on, proclaiming my demand, broad-cast, among each group I discovered, until a little sickly old man, with his face swollen and tied round, like Mrs. Siddons in *Lady Macbeth*, came out of a corner, where he was brooding over a ciga-rette, and looked at me pensively for some moments. He then took my passport and its accompanying note, and went away. I waited about three-quarters of an hour, and then thought it might be as well to see after him, and, by dint of exceeding pan-tomime and loud elocution, I contrived to send a reluctant clerk after him. Shortly afterwards the little old man came back, obviously finishing his dinner, a meal which I trust had been sweetened to him by the contemplation of my passport, and the thought that the owner was wasting his afternoon waiting for it. He signed to me to follow him, and took me into another room, strongly savoured by the meal he had been making, and sitting down he began to scrawl what it seems was a petition on my part. It took him half an hour, and caused him much per-plexity, but it consisted only of about eight lines, in the com-position of which he laid his head nearly flat upon the table, followed the formation of the letters with his tongue, grunted heavily, and generally worked as if he was undergoing a great labour. Four or five of his friends came in to help and advise him, and each in turn read his work, and ridiculed it until he became exasperated, and was going to destroy it, when I stopped him, and made him understand that I thought rather well of the performance. This seemed to give him comfort; he pushed his friends away, and indicated that I was to sign the work, which I did, though to this hour I have no idea of what I peti-tioned for. I can only hope it was nothing compromising my allegiance to the British constitution. He then took me across a large and most filthy yard, in which the ordinary mud of Odessa was amalgamated with the outpourings of a variety of offices, and conducted me up a flight of steps (at the very bottom of which he pulled off his hat) to a wooden lobby, along which the remains of somebody else's dinner were being carried by a barelegged girl, and so I presume the place was somebody's residence. Then he vanished, signing to me to un-

cover my head, while I waited in the lobby of dignity; but this
did not seem to me necessary, the less that the day was bitterly
cold.　In a short time he re-appeared, and took me again over
the filthy yard, and back to the bureau, where he demanded
certain rubles for items which I caused him to write down.
Then he demanded something for himself, but refused to give the
slightest idea of what were his notions of guerdon.　I concluded
that I had given him rather too much, because at first he made a
bow and seemed pleased; and then, as I was turning to go, he
held out the money, and looked abjectly at me, asking for more,
according to the Russian custom—pay what you will; but I
learned afterwards that I had hit within a few kopecs of the
proper remuneration.　He then sulkily told me to come again
in four days—a time he denoted by saying "Ponidilnik" and
"Vtornik," words by which I have reason to think he may have
meant Monday or Tuesday.　He further explained himself by
exhibiting for my inspection four of the dirtiest fingers I have
seen in Russia.

It appears that what is termed "publication" was the object
of the ceremony I had undergone.　Before leaving Russia, every
body is compelled to advertise himself, and the place to which
he is going, three times, in a newspaper of the locality in which
he has resided.　I had therefore to appear three times in the
journal to which I have alluded in a former letter—the *Journal
d'Odessa*—once in its Russian, and twice in its French impression.
The nominal reason for such publication is that a man may not
leave debts behind him, and therefore it might be expected that
some pains should be taken to procure an accurate description of
the traveller, that at least an interested person may not be
brought from some distant place, post haste, to stop insolvent
Robert Tomkins, when the real man who has advertised is honest
Richard Timkins.　Whether the Russians spell every body's
name as carefully as they did mine, I cannot say.　All I know
is, that I eagerly consulted the little pages of the original and
impetuous journal in question, and morning after morning I
found, after a string of announcements, that the Emperor had
turned this doctor into a *conseiller d'état,* and assured that colonel

that his men were in excellent order; and, after a mass of miserable imitation of Jules Janin,'in the shape of criticism upon a couple of fourth-rate *prime donne*, just then afflicting Odessa, that my petition had been granted, and my Odessa creditors were put on the alert. But as I scarcely recognised my own name in the mis-spelling—they had contrived to be wrong in the initial, and five other letters out of a dozen—the alertness ought to be very great indeed. I half conceive myself to have got out of Russia under some other gentleman's name.

This gentleman having been published three times, I, having paid for the process, went to the police to claim the benefit of it. Nobody knew any thing about the matter, as before, but I hunted up some of the friends of the little old man (who did not appear), and as they had great opportunities of examining me upon the former occasion, and had availed themselves thereof, they remembered me, and fetched somebody else, who fetched another person, who looked at me for a good while, and then went to a huge pile of papers, and pretended to hunt for a portion thereof. He went all through these papers three times, and then declared that the passport was not ready, and that I must come next day. On the other hand, I remarked that it ought to be ready, and that I should remain where I was until I had it, and to make this clearer (though as this man spoke French there was no mistake), I took a chair which stood beside some other official's desk, and placed it in a comfortable corner, sat down, and took out *Punch*. In two minutes he found my passport, which was second from the top of the heap. I was subsequently informed that I could have obtained the same result another way—namely, by putting my hand into my pocket, in which case the passport would have been produced at the first inspection; but that, not giving a fee to which the *employé* had no right, I was fortunate in not having had to make four journeys to the bureau, as happened to an unlucky Swiss, my neighbour at the hotel.

Having obtained the police passport, I had to go back to the governor's, where, as before, every thing presented a marked contrast to the police system. Civility and intelligence characterised every *employé* with whom I had any thing to do. A further delay, however, was necessary, and another visit. The time lost by this passport work is uncountable.

I attended again, when a fresh passport was drawn up, describing me with the usual catalogue of eyes, hair, height, &c., and which always seems useless, except in the case of some remarkable personal characteristic. Then two other statements concerning me were written into books which I had to sign, and I also signed some separate paper, and then flattered myself that I might say, as Elliston used to observe when he had silenced a claimant by accepting a bill, " Now, thank Heaven, *that* matter is off my mind for ever!" It *was* self-flattery.

I went to buy my ticket, entitling me to go to Constantinople. These tickets are sold in a room in the Custom-house, a propinquity which made me begin to be dubious as to results. The clerk immediately demanded my passport. This *did* seem to me absurd. " What on earth has the ticket-clerk of a steam-boat to do with my passport?" I said; but I had learned in Russia that the shortest way to get what you want is generally to do as you are bid. So I produced it. That was not it—he wanted my paper last given me at the governor's. Luckily I could produce that, too. He looked at it, and at me. I think he was going to give me my ticket, when it occurred to him to turn the paper over. Immediately he shut up his book of *coupons*. Where were the other signatures? What others did he want? " What others!" he repeated—not rudely, but as compassionating my ignorance—" why, you must get the signature of the captain of the quarantine, and the signature of the officer of the *douane*, and you must also get the signature of an officer of the Board of Health. Without those, I dare not give you this ticket—come another day."

It is not, perhaps, necessary to detail the tedious process of obtaining the three additional signatures to the testimonial of my being a fit person to be let out of Russia. The captain, and the doctor, and the *douanier* were all very polite, and, armed with their autographs, I made another attempt upon the ticket-vender, this time with success. I confess I did not suppose that even the tenacity of Russian hospitality could lime another twig to prevent my departure. It is ordered that voyagers shall be on board at least an hour before the time appointed for the steamer to start, and I was punctual—that is to say, I drove into the quarantine, whence the embarking takes place, about three o'clock in the afternoon. My charioteer—he deserves the title, considering the terrific pace at which he lashed his horses down the steep streets—was suddenly brought up by a tremendous shout from a cluster of officials, waiting in a kind of warehouse on the road—and my luggage was snatched from the car and laid upon the ground. The officials then resumed a conversation which my passage had interrupted, and, as this did not seem to have a direct bearing upon my voyage, I begged to know how long I was to be kept. One of them, after a pause, informed me that my luggage must be weighed. This was reasonable enough, and my only demand was why they did not weigh it—a remark which struck them, I suppose, for they only finished a few anecdotes, which made them all laugh heartily, and then one of them flung my modest packages into a huge scale. I am bound to say that I expected some charge, and watched the scale narrowly, but I happened to be, in point of luggage, an ounce or two under the allowed weight, and so they walked off. As nobody seemed to have any thing to say, my driver, who had been enraged at the epithets which had accompanied the order to stop, indignantly rushed at the trunk and desk, and replaced them. As we drove off, I think a demand was made for a fee for weighing, but as I am not quite sure of this, and, as I am quite sure that none was paid, I give the officers the benefit of the doubt. We entered the main enclosure, and, after a few trifling mistakes—such as my driver placing the boxes, first in a coal-yard, and then at the door of a soldier's station, to the exceeding rage of the sentinel —I was safely housed in the first portion of a shed, beyond which was a large room, fenced from us by gratings, and the further side of which was also formed of gratings. I could see another smaller grated room behind this, and beyond all I caught sight of the bright blue sea, with a number of masts dancing and flags fluttering.

This began to look like business, and I discharged my man
with a cheerful heart—an advantage I sought to put into his
possession by a few kopecs over his legitimate fare, and he
scarcely grumbled enough to keep up his national character.
The scene around me was lively enough. Almost all nations
were represented, in great force, if not in great respectability.
Several Turks — large, coarse, sensual-looking men — were
squatted on the ground, talking bad Italian to anybody who
would speak to them, and recreating themselves with the vast,
juicy, but flavourless melon of the country. Nearly all of them
had carpets, beds, pillows, and brass kettles, rolled together in
huge bundles, from which I concluded that they were to be deck
passengers. They had young boys with unwholesome-looking
countenances with them, and there was a Turkish woman who
religiously avoided the gaze of the infidels by keeping her *yash-
macc* close over her face, and by squatting, with her back towards
us, in the dirtiest corner of the little yard upon which the shed
opened. Eager Armenians were driving their last bargains, and
various Jews, with keen glances and long black gowns, were at
the same work, but with even greater intensity of interest. One
of them was very anxious to do a little business with me—What
money had I got?—I was going among the Turks, and should
want piastres and paras—he would give me some; and he almost
forced his hand into my pocket to obtain my rubles, for which
he swore he would give me better exchange than any man in
Europe or Asia, for he loved the English. And as I did not
avail myself of his kindness, he came back, after a short time,
and said that the Black Sea was very cold—I had not half
enough clothing, and he happened, by the express blessing of
Luck, to know a friend who had a lovely fur cloak, which I
should have for about a tenth of what it was worth. *Fur—
homo trium literarum*, I muttered, but the Hebrew did not heed,
and finally offered me an amber mouth-piece for my cigar. Why
did I smoke without a mouth-piece? and incontinently he pulled
one out of a greasy pocket, and desired me to try how beautifully
it fitted my mouth. Again repulsed, I do not know what else
he would have tempted me with, but that he was called off by

an accomplice, who directed him to a more promising customer. The busy crowd thickened, various Odessa merchants came down, as did a cluster of women, to take farewells, and some dark-eyed Italians, who were going with us, and had dreadful fights with their avaricious drosky-drivers, in which some words sounding sadly like *diavolo* and *inferno* came into great play. Presently the epaulettes of the quarantine officer glittered among the mob, and his white-coated followers cleared him a passage up to the door of the first grating. He immediately turned us all out of the shed into the yard, where we crowded together with great friendliness, and he sent in men to clear the large apartment of which I have spoken. What quantities of fruit, chiefly lemons, they staggered away with for some half-hour, it were difficult to estimate, but the place teemed with odours, which, under the circumstances, were peculiarly refreshing. This ceremony ended, the officer called his subordinates around him, and they formed a sort of vista, at the end of which he took his station, and demanded the passports of passengers. These were handed in to him with a rush, as petitions are fluttered up from all sides to the table of the House of Commons, and he inspected them severally, with great attention, and put several aside, as incomplete, to the dismay of those therein named. Mine was among these; so I pushed my way through the soldiers, and required to know what was the matter with my precious paper. He thrust it to me without speaking, but a man at my elbow said, " There's another signature wanting."

If they had told me to go to St. Petersburg, and obtain the hand-writing of the Emperor (" the Autograph of All the Russians," as Mrs. Ramsbottom called him), I should hardly have been more astonished. I looked round to see whose signature I should ask, at random. Any body who would have favoured me with his hand should have done so. But a soldier observed my state of mind, and quietly withdrawing himself from the *cordon*, signed to me to give him the paper, and disappeared. I followed him, and he entered a low building in the neighbourhood, in which he remained so long that I began to apprehend some new stratagem to detain me in the country.

But after I had battered at the door a good many times, he came out, apparently without any paper, but intimated that "all was right." As he did not produce the document, I was not so sure of this, and luckily espying a man whom I had heard speaking Russian, I requested him to demand the paper. After a few words, he said, "He thinks you ought to give him a small present." "Let him give me my passport, first," I said; upon which hint the fellow produced it from the breast of his coat. I snatched it away, and hurried to the officer, who was pleased to say that it would do. What the soldier got put upon it I never knew, but he had earned the ten kopecs I threw to him. The officer then directed that I should be let into the large apartment, into which I went, dragging my trunk after me. I was locked in, and was fairly in quarantine. Nothing now could take me out on the land side—I felt that I was a dangerous person, and associated with plague localities. In that grated cell I was kept a long time, and five or six others, cabin passengers, were also let in. We could see sailors clustering on the sea-side, and apparently waiting to take us away. After about half an hour, during which nothing seemed to be done outside, the officer let himself in, locked the door, and filtered us through into the further chamber, calling out our names—queerly mutilated, from the passports, which he gave to us as we passed through. Then we were locked in the last room, but we could see two large boats—one for luggage, the other for us—jumping up and down by the quay. Another long wait, and the last door was opened, the sailors rushed frantically upon our luggage and hurled it into the boats; some of us sprang in wildly after it, utterly refusing to be dislodged, and defying all the world; and finally we shoved off in a very mutinous state, and in ten minutes were alongside the Cherson steam-boat. Our passports were then taken from us for the very last time of asking, and in another hour we were out of Odessa Bay, and those who were subject to such affections were yielding to the antibilious effects of the long, dangerous swell of the Black Sea.

Such is the process of getting out of Russia. I have described it exactly as it took place, without a particle of exaggeration.

Any one who is good at arithmetic can sum up the number of hours likely to be wasted in obtaining the number of signatures required; and any one who is equally good· at practical philosophy can sum up the advantages which any body, except a mob of *employés*, gains by the system. I need not say that there is a goodly quantity of fees coming out of the operation, to say nothing of bribery (which on this occasion I had resolved not to employ) to expedite it. To the poor, this must be no small addition to the heavy expense of travelling in this part of the world. But I have nothing to do with results—my object here, as elsewhere, has been merely to state facts, or to record the sentiments of those affected by them. The passport system is most rigidly enforced, and any idea of breaking through any of its nets or their smallest meshes is only paralleled by Mr. Wyndham's celebrated illustration of a certain proposed *coup de main*—"You might as well talk of a *coup de main* in the Court of Chancery."

Before leaving Odessa, I availed myself of almost the only opportunity which my occupations allowed me of making a visit which had no connection with the business on which I entered Russia. The kindness of a friend procured me admission to the magnificent house in which, to the great regret of the city, Prince Woronzow's important duties forbid his often being a resident, although the mansion itself is kept in perfect order and readiness for its owner's reception. The house stands on the best site in the town, and is nearly the first object on which the eye of the spectator rests as he approaches from the sea. It is rendered still more striking by an entirely detached colonnade on one side, consisting of a double row of bold and lofty columns, which, rising from the elevated cliff, invest with a classical character the earliest impressions of the place. The house is very spacious, and commands a superb view of the whole port, and a fine lookout to sea. The entrance is in an extensive court-yard, on one side of which is a building so elegant in its form that it is necessary to enter it to discover that it is simply a range of stables. Opposite is the house, which forms an angle, and takes nearly the whole of two sides of the court. The arrangement of the rooms is very good, and the ornaments comprise numerous specimens

of rare and valuable productions of various countries, while the
walls are decorated with a choice collection of pictures, chiefly
formed by the prince's father, so long known and so highly
esteemed in England, where he resided as ambassador. Among
the more striking ornaments is a magnificent gold vase, of very
large dimensions, presented to the prince as a military recognition, and another vase of great size, in malachite, one of the most
beautiful specimens of this stone I have ever seen. A collection
of busts of royal and distinguished personages, chiefly, I understood,
presents from the originals, are likewise here, as also marble copies
from many of the more famous works of ancient art. One of
these was pointed out to me as having been curiously affected
by one of the earthquakes which have been sustained by Odessa
—it was not thrown from its pedestal, as might have been expected, but was turned nearly round, with its face from the
spectator. Large full-lengths of the recent Sovereigns of Russia,
by eminent artists, are among the adornments of the house, and
in particular I was interested by a masterly picture of Catherine
the Second, in which the artist, while preserving the portraiture
of a very fine and almost captivating woman—flesh, blood, and
animation—has not shrunk from indicating, with great truthful-
ness, certain other characteristics of this strange creature, which
history has recorded with a less artistic severity. An admirable
portrait of Mr. Pitt, with the motto, *Non sibi sed patriæ*, hangs
perhaps in a less advantageous light than so fine a work deserves,
but it cannot be passed over by the most careless spectator.
There are, indeed, numberless recollections of England throughout
the mansion; and I was much pleased to see on the children's
shelves the soundest and best of the works of Miss Edgeworth
and Maria Hack. It is almost trespassing on fairy ground to
describe the *boudoir* of the Princess Woronzow, with its charming
demijour, half due to exquisite coloured glass, and half to the
towering tenants of the spacious conservatory upon which it looks.
The prince's own cabinet, with its collection of philosophical instruments, might perhaps be a more legitimate subject for description, were one writing for that purpose, and not merely
recording a most pleasant visit. The library contains but a

comparatively small portion of Prince Woronzow's collection of books, but it comprises a large mass of valuable works, and includes not only the oldest but the newest of our own most valued authors. It was more than agreeable to withdraw for an hour from the examination of a system and the collection of details, and to find myself suddenly in the midst of evidences, not so much of the power of wealth and rank to accumulate elegant luxuries, and to appropriate honourable testimonials, as of the exercise of taste and intellect in the selection of the real treasures of art and literature.

That, in regard to the latter department at least, there is no very strong sympathy among Russian officials, was evidenced under my observation at the Custom-house. A gentleman who had recently returned to Russia had some months previously sent home a number of books, in various languages, and these had been, of course, stopped at the *douane.* On his arrival, he set himself to work to get them through, and was in many instances successful, despite the great severity of the censorship. This "censure" appeared to me to work exceedingly harshly, except in the case of the deserved condemnation of immoral books, which, however, though rigorously proscribed, are continually introduced under cover of most virtuous titles and letterings. In the present instance, the owner of the books sought to be brought in was particularly anxious to obtain some Swedish works which were among them. But these were as pertinaciously denied him. He vainly demanded some reason for the exclusion, and explained that they were all of the most blameless character, having nothing to do either with religion politics, or morals. All was of no use—he could not have them. Again he desired to know whether any of them were specifically objected to, as he could not imagine that all Swedish works were prescribed in a mass. No explanation was afforded him, but that the books would not be given up—that was all. But he reminded the officials that, some months before, they had actually passed a number of Swedish books for him—what did the change mean? His perseverance began to offend the authorities, and he got no other answer but the preceding one, a little more tartly given.

But he finally obtained some light on the point, for one day he contrived to gain a sight of some of his Swedish books, with the word *Inconnu* over the batch. Upon this hint he represented to the officials that he had become aware that they knew nothing about the books one way or the other, and that they should endeavour to be enlightened, and he begged them to read the books. Out it came at last, that, there being a censorship for the examination of books, and the condemnation of such as were immoral, that censorship comprised nobody who understood a word of Swedish, or could give an opinion on the subject. So that Swedish literature—and the admirers of Jenny Lind and Frederica Bremer may as well know it—is at present excluded from the south of Russia, and the national lyrics of the one and the national novels of the other must not be sent to that discourteous market.

It is also due to Odessa to mention that it is not altogether unaware of some of its deficiencies, and especially of its want of decent lighting. And as far as setting up a few stalwart look-ing gas-lamps goes, in one part of the town, a step has been taken in the right direction. But there is a serious drawback to the utility of these lamps, in the fact that there is no gas, and no great chance of there being any. A few days before I left, how-ever, a sensation was caused by the rumour that on a given night gas was to flow into the pipes, and the town was to be in a blaze, and people promenaded in the hope of seeing the phenomenon, as in other countries they look for fireworks. Having walked until they were weary, and the fire not having appeared, I pre-sume they went home by oil-light, as they have done for many a long year. There was, I found upon inquiry, considerable foundation for the report, inasmuch as a gentleman of some theoretical knowledge, or at least ambition, on the subject of gas —but who, I was informed, had never seen either a gasometer or even a gas-light at all—had undertaken to illuminate the town upon a principle which he supposed to be new and good, but which turned out to be neither. He was, with commendable spirit, a good deal encouraged by the authorities, but the affair ended in disappointment. An English company, if they could be admitted, would have the town in one blaze of light in a quarter of a year; but this would not suit either systems or individuals, and an attempt of the kind, already made, was burked at the earliest outset.

I cannot conclude this series of letters on Russia without bearing testimony to the kind assistance which I have received from numerous gentlemen in the course of my inquiries, and without which aid, in a country like Russia, it would have been impossible for me to have carried out those inquiries. To record their names would be to violate promises which, however I may regret their necessity, I must keep, until released from them by those to whom they were made. But there is one case in which, happily, no such secresy is needed, and that is in the case of our own Consul-General, Mr. James Yeames. To that gentleman's earnest interest in the object I had in view—to his sound and practical advice, founded upon the experience of more than a quarter of a century in Russia—and to much invaluable information afforded by him upon statistical matters, I am most happy thus to record my debt.

THE END.

M'CORQUODALE AND CO., PRINTERS, LONDON.—
WORKS, NEWTON.

CPSIA information can be obtained
at www.ICGtesting.com
Printed in the USA
LVHW080509121020
668563LV00005B/140